I AM THE ARROW

ALSO BY SARAH RUDEN

Vergil: The Poet's Life

Paul Among the People

The Face of Water

Other Places

TRANSLATIONS

The Gospels

Confessions: Augustine

The Greek Plays: Sixteen Plays by Aeschylus, Sophocles, and Euripides (Agamemnon, Libation Bearers, Eumenides)

Hippias Minor or the Art of Cunning

The Golden Ass: Apuleius

The Aeneid: Vergil

Homeric Hymns

Aristophanes: Lysistrata

Petronius: Satyricon

I Am the Arrow

THE LIFE AND ART OF SYLVIA PLATH
IN SIX POEMS

Sarah Ruden

LIBRARY OF AMERICA

Published in the United States by Library of America.
Visit our website at www.loa.org.

Distributed to the trade in the United States by
Penguin Random House Inc. and in Canada by
Penguin Random House Canada Ltd.

Library of Congress Control Number: 2024949944
ISBN 978–1–59853–813–7

1 3 5 7 9 10 8 6 4 2

Printed in the United States of America

Contents

I AM THE ARROW

Introduction

IT IS EASY to spot important poetry: the words, it's said, leap off the page. The poems of Sylvia Plath's literary maturity are like this. In "The Applicant," an interview starts off very badly. A silent figure is rebuffed by an interviewer for lack of all the outward signs of being "our sort of a person": from a glass eye to "stitches to show something's missing," not one requisite is in evidence. The interviewer then becomes an impatient salesperson:

> Stop crying.
> Open your hand.
> Empty? Empty. Here is a hand
>
> To fill it and willing
> To bring teacups and roll away headaches
> And do whatever you tell it.
> Will you marry it?

The abrupt commands and the one-word question (asked only to be answered by the asker) attack the applicant's helpless show of emotion. This is the diction of a school principal or policeman who has caught someone in the act; but then expansive manipulation leads to the shocking question, "Will you marry it?" By the time the voice talks up a black suit that will last a lifetime and calls a servile "living doll" out of a closet to fill the applicant's allegedly empty head, the social commentary is undeniable.

Plath has often passed for more of a political cause than a poet, a judgment that reduces her reach into new readerships and frustrates lucid judgment of her aesthetics. But the problem with bewailing this impression of her is how freighted Plath actually was—and how she freighted her work in turn—with conflicts heavier than those of personal tragedy, conflicts that were social and historical, and thus public issues, active all around her and pressing in on her; that *did* invite her to resist everything around her; that *do* lure us to take her side, almost as if she were still alive and could, like a living person, find victory.

Her father, Otto, was a German immigrant in America who was repeatedly sent back by bigotry to square one in his education and work. An extreme jaw-setting striver, he finally acquired a professorship and a family, but he was betrayed by a long habit of resisting others' judgments of him and pressing forward without help. He died from diabetes treated too late, because for months he had kept his mistaken self-diagnosis of incurable cancer to himself. He was leery of insurance salesmen as well as doctors, and so left his family in danger of destitution. His daughter was only eight at the time, and over the years took from her struggling, self-sacrificing, ailing, resentful mother, Aurelia, the same lesson that had doomed her father: there was safety only in knuckling-down and isolating perfection. Mid-twentieth-century misogyny was happy to press its own version of this formula on Plath, and by her junior year in college she found herself in overwhelming depression, which was treated by a brutal early version of electroshock—part of a system of medically taming troublesome people—especially women—to which her own paternal grandmother was perhaps subjected. (Ernestine Plath's husband committed her to a mental institution as "insane," and she died there years later, but evidence of psychosis in her medical records seems weak; she was likely just depressed or suffering from early-onset dementia, or both.) Then in England, as a student, wife, and mother, and as an author on a strenuous rise, Plath had to contend with even harsher attitudes toward women, with anti-Americanism, and with the rigors of postwar austerity that clung on. It was naturally much harder when her close, collaborative marriage to the British poet Ted Hughes failed, leaving her painfully exposed and helplessly enraged, with two small children to care for. It would be surprising if, during her last months, she had not depicted the world as merciless or indifferent, in particular toward women.

Sometimes Plath's work is explicitly political. In

her intimately autobiographical novel, *The Bell Jar*, she has a lot to say about the dehumanizing treatment she endured from all sides as a bright, ambitious— and eventually suicidal—college girl. "The Applicant," written during the crisis of a decade later, when Hughes accused her of trying to enslave him to domesticity, makes it clear that she thought there was plenty of dehumanization to go around: by hurting women, it hurt men too. And it was established, cultural, organizational; another poem, "Death & Co.," makes that claim in its title.

One major snag in claiming Plath for political causes, however, is the impulse to call her a feminist, as the feminist movement we know did not exist for her. (Betty Friedan's *The Feminine Mystique* was published about a week after Plath's death.) Whereas in other matters she was leftist to a boring degree, Plath was ambivalent or even hostile toward powerful, independent, undomestic women, including her own mentors; she devoted herself to ancillary support of her husband's career, cooked, gardened, sewed clothes for her children, and painted hearts and flowers on her furniture.

On February 11, 1963, Plath killed herself in a London flat where she had been living with her children. Personal partisanship and politics dogged even the parts of her afterlife that for other authors are strictly literary. Hughes's posthumous treatment of her archive and memory gave rise to decades of controversy, a key issue always being whether in her chilling fury against him, the woman with whom he had been having an affair, and other figures and forces, Plath was protesting cogently or raving. This issue has variously colored the proliferating, in some cases feverishly debated, biographies of Plath and the memoirs of people who knew her.

In presenting this selection of her poems, I will be arguing for Plath's establishment, on purely literary merit, in the cool mainstream of literary greatness, which verges toward political tolerance and open-mindedness. The culminating work Plath left has kept—and in fact increased—its appeal for more than sixty years, despite fashions of self-expression and both public and private concerns shifting at a rate never known before. A poem like "The Applicant" can be Exhibit A in the suit for her rights as an *author*, whose *words* fascinate us and draw our minds to common, enduring elements of the human condition—in this poem, our propensity to treat each other like things, among other realities. "Mythmaker" is a byword for Plath, but in her case the full meaning of the term has not been appreciated. She was certainly well enough in control of her own persona to cast a populous, bewitching, and bewildering drama out of her single living self: at different times she projected a golden girl, a vamp, a devoted daughter and wife, a domestic goddess, a bitch goddess, an earth mother, a poor mental patient, and a woman martyr. But by "myth," both ancient Greek authors and modern anthropologists mean not illusion but accepted and guiding truth for a whole society. Best known through traditional mythologies, myth not only imparts the lessons of a particular shared experience but also makes claims about the nature of experience; and thus over time myth can appeal to more and more people who have less and less in common. Plath was a mythmaker in this more important sense.

As a PhD student in the eighties, I used to sneak into the twentieth-century American literature stacks in Harvard's Widener Library and sit on the floor reading Plath when I was supposed to be studying Greek and Roman authors for my qualifying exams. I had little in common with her beyond that she was a poet and I wanted to be one. Plath could not even get into Frank O'Connor's summer creative writing class at Harvard, and the rejection helped precipitate her suicide attempt. I could be a doctoral student at Harvard because in my generation attitudes toward ambitious women were very different; in fact, my father (who was, if anything, excessively present in my life) told me I had more than a right to all my opportunities, as women were natural professionals who should be running the world. But did I ever want reassurance about something general, the possibility of rising above suffering, and Plath gave me that. In great writing, the medium is the message of the myth: transcendence, permanence.

As a classicist by training and a translator of ancient

languages (Latin, Greek, Hebrew) by profession, I am comfortable with ideas of striving genius and artistic immortality that may seem hidebound in this era, and in the case of most well-known modern authors admittedly may be so. The ancient conception of the heights of Parnassus is far more practical and less pretentious than the Romantic idea of the author as an unaccountable force of nature and a living reproach to convention and conformity, an idea that is still quite influential today. The ancients held that, whatever an aspirant's talents and character might be, the indispensable thing was to perfect a linguistic craft within a literary tradition so that the resulting compositions would last. Horace, the fat little Roman freedman, glories in his lyric *Odes* (whose impossible-seeming adaptations of Greek meters sing like birds) with the line *exegi monumentum aere perennius*: "I have completed a memorial more enduring than bronze." Sylvia Plath too was preoccupied with monumentality, and—in the poem "Edge," particularly—produced memorable images of the poet as a permanent, looming artifact; no wonder, as through her writing she turned her body, her mind, her experiences, her *self* into rooted, weighty objects.

I also bring to these works' vivid intricacies a classicist's—and a translator's—habit of hovering over the original texts, of concentrating on how these words work. I share, too, the late-antique interest in the biography of genius; I'm riveted by the question of how mere human beings can achieve so much. In any event,

Plath's life has to be considered, as she was a deeply autobiographical author. For the essays in this book I often draw on Plath biographies and on the autobiographical novel *The Bell Jar*. My proviso, however, is that this life seems to me most informative as a *literary* life. Plath was, though not multilingual, a creature of language, of words, to an extent that has been rare since the Renaissance, and common only in late antiquity, when rhetoric defined education. She was taught from the cradle to love words by a mother who had insisted on earning a master's in English after her training as a secretary. She proved to have an excellent but idiosyncratic ear—all punch and rhythm but no melody, no comfortable softness or sweetness as in a stereotypical female poet. (She was in fact tone-deaf and could play the piano only mechanically.) Plath drew on her gift for mimicry, and often used what she picked up from her social interchanges and from overheard speech. She satirized her culture's exalted hucksters, as in "The Applicant" ("A living doll, everywhere you look"). She inserted her voice into the patterns of playground chants by which some of the least powerful in society strut and attack, as in "Daddy," with its long-u rhymes running through its flippantly furious sixteen stanzas. She listened to the words around her and in herself, and adopted and adapted them.

Plath also studied under Wilbury Crockett, a momentously gifted high school English teacher, in his rigorous three-year-long literature seminar. She excelled as a literature student at Smith, and as a Fulbright scholar at Cambridge she anxiously attended to what she considered gaps in her knowledge, including ancient and Shakespearean tragedy. Awed by her husband's trust in poetic instinct and taking on his rural, folkloric, and occult interests as new inspirations, she sat across the table from him day by day as they both composed, and listened to his criticisms. She participated in Robert Lowell's poetry workshop at Harvard along with Anne Sexton, imbibing the then-fashionable confessional ethos at first hand, and tried to apprentice herself to Marianne Moore, the leading American woman poet of the time, with her syllabic verse (which eschews a traditional metrical beat), precise imagery, and cerebral distance. (Moore's "Poetry" begins, "I too, dislike it.") Theodore Roethke was another poet Plath imitated and sought to enlist as a patron, this time successfully. She had a number of other influences, including contemporary British poets like Norman Nicholson. But in spite of—or as a reaction against?—her compulsive acolyte moves, it was eventually Plath who wrote works that were to remain both a preoccupation of scholars and cultishly popular. And in the history of women's self-expression, her work was outright epochal.

Plath was not a cool, ethical observer of romantic coupling, wifehood, and motherhood, standing outside of these things like Jane Austen, or outside the conventional family like Virginia Woolf. She was not an experienced partisan of women's traditional fate either, like Elizabeth Barrett Browning, or someone with no personal interest in it, like Willa Cather. She was not a victim of eroticism, like Katherine Mansfield, or of domesticity, like Shirley Jackson. And she was not like the more recent authors for whom questions of women's choices and their consequences shrank to manageable size where their own lives were concerned: Margaret Atwood and Toni Morrison are examples. No: Plath both created and embodied the Homeric or Vergilian myth of womanhood, of the hero who has been to the underworld and seen the unspeakable realities, yet speaks of them; she became both the image and the reality of the woman warrior who, like Camilla, fights the losing battle to the end and triumphs through her undying fame. This is why so many readers have long regarded her as something more than just an author, why her story seems to have a significance touching on the metaphysical.

This does not mean that I consider Plath a magical being. To me she is more impressive as a human being who had to struggle long and hard, especially in acquiring her knowledge and skills. As a sometime teacher of creative writing, I dread aspiring poets reading this, but early on, Plath tried too hard, was too diligent a student, too elaborate a craftswoman, and too good a mimic when she was imitating prevailing styles. She published in newspapers and magazines from the age of eight, she could not notice the weather without rehearsing metaphors, she abused *Roget's Thesaurus* like a drug, and by the time she came of age she was prepared to turn out an appalling villanelle—the show-piece form of the era—called "To Eva Descending the Stair," decorating with a mass of devices the overdone theme of innocence and initiation. "Red the unraveled rose sings in your hair," goes one line.

She did not break through until around a decade later, and that seems to have come mainly from the opportunity to sit still; she vindicated Virginia Woolf's *A Room of One's Own*, which deplored the conditions under which women had always struggled to create, as deadly for their equal innate genius. At the artists' colony Yaddo in Saratoga, New York, Plath was thoroughly well cared for, for the first time since toddlerhood. The severe illness of her infant brother, two and a half years younger than she, and not her father's death, began her hardships. As a half orphan, Plath actually shared a room with her mother, an arrangement that continued into her adulthood. She spent much of her honeymoon cooking and cleaning in a primitive rental on the Spanish coast, having married the most talented man she knew, who was nearly penniless. At Yaddo she nervously gloried in free time, openhanded material provisions, and quiet, pleasant surroundings. She wrote, among other clear advances from her previous work, "Mushrooms," the first of her mature object poems. ("Poppies in July" and "Cut" are a couple of the later ones.) "Mushrooms" is a pocket ironic horror movie in which insensate, tiny, fragile things are set to take over the world.

In "You're," Plath, back in England, addresses her first pregnancy with tender humor and a welter of animal, plant, geographic, and festival imagery, her imagination reveling in the unaccountable and separate life within her that is more beloved for her already letting go of it. In contrast to these jewels of poetry flashing just a few facets, "The Babysitters" is a letter-like piece of nostalgia addressed to a college friend who worked near Plath when both were au pairs for wealthy families summering on the Massachusetts coast. The poem illustrates why *The Bell Jar* is Plath's best-selling work: the narrator of both is a young person in a tortuous eddy of her development that seems more vivid in memory than it would have been in life; this is the effect of Plath's sardonic, colloquial verve in mimicking her young self. "And the seven-year-old wouldn't go out unless his jersey stripes / Matched the stripes of his socks," snarks the poem.

These three poems are my selections from Plath's earlier masterpieces; "Mushrooms" appears in *The Colossus* (1960), the only collection published while the poet was still alive. The speaker in the title poem of the collection is a stranded, Robinson Crusoe–like caretaker of a hopelessly derelict, impossibly massive fallen statue—Plath's father, but also all kinds of pinioning, exhausting authority, including the authority of her own habits and expectations. A flip of the topos coin is the late "Gulliver," in which the speaker is the giant, tethered-down figure, tormented by the tiny, busy creatures all over it.

"Gulliver" belongs to Plath's posthumous collection *Ariel* (1965), without which none of us would have heard of her. ("You're," though relatively early, is also an *Ariel* poem; "The Babysitters" belongs to *Crossing the Water*, published in 1971.) From among the *Ariel* poems of Plath's last few months, I chose three for this book: "The Applicant"; "Ariel," with its self-sacrificial ecstatic release; and the solemnly triumphant "Edge," the last or second-to-last poem of her life.

At the end of my weeks-long, climb-the-walls anxieties in choosing from among the all-important last three and a half years of Plath's work, I arrived at a more even time-of-composition spread than might be expected, but not in deference to the biographical story that, at one level, the poems tell, and certainly not in an effort to explain, by comparisons of the poems over time, her most famous and characteristic work as a psychic or spiritual epiphany brought on by her husband's affair, his departure, and all the accompanying stresses, which included the severe depression to which she succumbed. One reason I reject this scenario is that the huge gathering of facts about Plath, culminating in Heather Clark's magnificent 2020 biography *Red Comet*, gives little support to it. The idea of this late implosive flowering seems to

exist mainly because Hughes—under fire for his lucra-
tive farming of her archive (he owned everything, as
they were not divorced) and his editing and destruc-
tion of documents to obviate the criticisms, doubts,
and rage that she had directed toward him from the
start of their marriage—conducted a decades-long
campaign of self-justification that depended on an *Ariel*
legend: that Plath's pathology had swept her beyond
her marriage, beyond all human help, and into witchy
heights of infuriated genius consubstantial with sui-
cide. No matter that the depression leading to Plath's
first, very serious suicide attempt rendered her unable
to write at all, and that the depression leading to what
may have been a mere suicidal gesture (intended to
extort a hospital bed for herself more quickly?) saw
her writing exquisitely within a few days of her death:
the legend conformed to the Romantics' and confes-
sionalists' association of art with disease (tuberculosis,
madness) and played well with a public that liked to
imagine such a shortcut to creativity and fame; and it
allowed the male literary establishment that had con-
descended to Plath, and even rejected submissions of
poems that went on to become classics, to deprecate
her in memory. The poet and editor Al Alvarez, in *The
Savage God*, memorializes Plath not as a powerful writer
as much as a suicidal one, and depicts her in her final
months as a sort of emotional and literary waif he did
his best to help. But millions of people are depressed,
and hundreds of thousands commit suicide. There was

only one Sylvia Plath the poet, and she became that because of her immense talent and her tireless refusal to make anything less than extraordinary out of it.

I believe there is no story to tell of a late, mad outburst into virtuosity, and this belief is reflected in the wide chronological distribution of my selection. From the start, I made an effort to consider quality only, and I continue to judge that the best of the poems from late 1962 and early 1963, the last months of her life, are only marginally better than the best from before then; and I find more of the earlier poems more purely pleasurable. I realize, of course, that the masterpieces I designate as "earlier" and "later" come from a poignantly short period, roughly the last three and a half years of a life only thirty years long. But I think it is important to take into account how well she was writing over that whole period in spite of awful circumstances during the last part of it, especially since the claim that she wrote better when and because she was losing her mind is insulting to her agency as a writer and defies common sense and experience: it is, like the belief that a person writes much better when drunk, or sleepwalking, or on peyote, not true. The personal crisis near the end of Plath's life did contribute to new and arresting kinds of expressiveness, but sometimes she opened herself up to serious questions of taste and ethics. "Daddy" is brilliant, but I understand why many people object to its invocation of the Holocaust in the context of an individual woman's self-destructive rage against her dead father. I myself can't surrender to the poem as fully as I would need to in order to include it in this collection.

The truth is that Plath sometimes craved sheer attention and could go for short-term fixes such as cinema-noir lines, like "I eat men like air" at the end of "Lady Lazarus," or whole melodramatic poems, like "Childless Woman," which is aimed at her romantic rival Assia Wevill. But real literary achievement is a deal made with readers of the future: "I have made something good enough that you will love it when no one gives a rat's ass about me, the living human being." In social gatherings, especially with tastemakers, Plath was apt to gush and pander, or remain cautiously silent; in courses she polished apples and imitated. The biographies attest that her greatest growth came when she was most alone and thus least self-conscious: at Yaddo, in a borrowed studio away from her young children for whole half-days, and on a country estate after her poet husband left her. In these places she learned to turn her self-concern inside out, to transform herself into the ghost, the eminence, the immanence, the myth, through words alone. That sounds lofty, and it was, but she could reach that height when she had the time and space to put herself together as an author, and could do it without interference: she had her talent, her learning, her work ethic, and her self-criticism, and her depression was no match for them.

Plath's triumph through language carries special warning and inspiration in the internet age. Words *need* the kind of care she gave them. They need to be invested with their full weight and seriousness, because they transform reality by performing in it. My favorite lines of Plath are in "Edge": "Her bare / Feet seem to be saying: / We have come so far, it is over." It is a paradox, of course. Because Plath came so far, it is definitely not over; it is in fact a lesson in hope, in the possibility of things not being ended, in their enduring against all the odds.

Mushrooms

NOVEMBER 13, 1959

Overnight, very
Whitely, discreetly,
Very quietly

Our toes, our noses
Take hold on the loam,
Acquire the air.

Nobody sees us,
Stops us, betrays us;
The small grains make room.

Soft fists insist on
Heaving the needles,
The leafy bedding,

Even the paving.
Our hammers, our rams,
Earless and eyeless,

Perfectly voiceless,
Widen the crannies,
Shoulder through holes. We

Diet on water,
On crumbs of shadow,
Bland-mannered, asking

Little or nothing.
So many of us!
So many of us!

We are shelves, we are
Tables, we are meek,
We are edible,

Nudgers and shovers
In spite of ourselves.
Our kind multiplies:

We shall by morning
Inherit the earth.
Our foot's in the door.

"**M**USHROOMS" is among the poems Sylvia Plath wrote during her stay, along with Ted Hughes, at the Yaddo artists' colony in Saratoga in the fall of 1959, after a year of teaching at her alma mater, Smith, and a hardscrabble cross-continental trip in a car borrowed from her mother. At Yellowstone, a bear smashed the back window and raided the food, lingering for the rest of the night while the couple hunkered down in their tent. A photo of Plath rowing in the national park in a bathing suit shows emaciated, vivid ribs stacked above evanescent breasts, and arms not much thicker than broom handles. Yaddo, with its cozy accommodations and excellent food, proved relaxing and invigorating like nothing before to Plath, who was pregnant with her first child. She strolled the grounds, browsed the library, had time to mull over problems and possibilities she was used to just shouldering through.

Delicious meals she did not have to shop for and cook were especially welcome to her. "As usual, our main news is that we are wellfed [sic]. . . . Last night it was juicy ham, pineapple (baked), sweet potatoes, corn, spinach, hot rolls, butter, and deep dish apple pie," she wrote to her mother. However, for Plath anxiety was never at bay long, and she was not yet putting it to best effect in her work. "Poem for a Birthday," in seven parts, is widely considered a Yaddo-enabled breakthrough, and a brilliant one, yet even there her very original mind is still hampered. She imprints herself on T. S. Eliot's "The Love Song of J. Alfred Prufrock" and *The Waste Land* and Theodore Roethke's "The Lost Son," with her cold-voiced catalog of disillusion, desolation, disintegration, viciousness, helplessness, grotesquerie. Under the heading of the final movement, "The Stones," she incants, "This is the city where men are mended. / I lie on a great anvil." The first line is like solemn Eliot and Roethke, the second is shocking Plath, with a metaphor of sexual violence now connected to the poem's complaint of an imprisoning marriage. This combination is impressive, but the movement is forty-five lines long and veers rather crazily back and forth between the body and the hellscape and its other inhabitants. Such a scene is quite different from what Plath has to communicate at her best and most original. There, even her supreme artistry is subordinate to her riveting message about the world's collision with her unstinting mind and her female body. Her most mature poems deliver to us a mighty, precise, and beautiful intensity, like a Picasso portrait of one of his lovers—a young woman like many others, but because she was *his*, and painted by *him*, her image makes the reader willing, indeed happy, to spend time in contemplation of it and to reconsider all sorts of things, including desire, possession, and fertility. This kind of achievement was where Plath was headed in late 1959, and at moments she would surpass her revered models. Readers were not going to say, "What a skillful, original, memorable poem," but would feel (as many do of Picasso), "She made herself into art, and made that art part of us." "Mushrooms" is a breakthrough in that direction.

This, to my mind, makes the immediate background to the genesis of "Mushrooms" important. The day before Plath wrote much of "Poem for a Birthday," she recorded in her journal that "Ted dreams of killing animals: bears, donkeys, kittens. Me or the baby?" On the day she had "miraculously" poured out not only "Birthday" but also the ingenious and posthumously much anthologized "Colossus" ("[both of which] I find colorful and amusing") and "The Manor Garden," she turned in the journal from satisfaction to gloom: "But my man-

uscript of my book seems dead to me." She spends the
rest of the paragraph hoping for and despairing of pub-
lication and prizes, and in the next paragraph deplores
the autobiographical focus and "monastery living" that
have in fact made her promising new work possible.
Then she turns to ambitious plans for study, including
painting and languages.

A few days later comes a quite different moment:
"Wrote an exercise on mushrooms yesterday which
Ted likes. And I do to [sic]. My absolute lack of judg-
ment when I've written something: whether it's trash
or genius." The three short sentences' brazen dou-
ble (or quadruple) consciousness (the primacy of her
husband's opinion to her; her piping up to second it,
but, it turns out, in much lengthier and stronger terms;
her "absolute lack of judgment"; and yet her immedi-
ate leap to extreme labels) might signal her biggest
breakthrough: she was starting to have fun, her own
kind of defiant and surmounting fun. In the section of
"Birthday" headed "The Beast," the mate is a "Mud-
sump, happy sty-face" in whose annihilating filth she
is trapped forever; in reality he was also her invaluable
partner and colleague, as she now lightly acknowl-
edges. And her own work inexorably provokes her
hatred or admiration but can somehow also now be
viewed dispassionately. She does not need to get bent
out of shape trying to wrestle conflicts to death but can
see what they offer to revel in. One paragraph down

in the journal, and she is going over implacable old guilt and resentment—but they now have a distinctly humorous twist from her subconscious: she dreamt of her mother and brother "in puritanical, harsh, snoopy poses," and her brother caught her in bed with "someone whose name was Partisan Review." This magazine, a powerful tastemaker, published one of Plath's poems that fall.

Plath spent untold time and effort trying to sort out the psychic and circumstantial dilemmas she felt kept her from excellence, and, failing that, to fit them into approved modes of modernism and confessionalism. But perhaps her greatest find was a sort of shrug: the discovery, in her poetry at least, that her best friend was her wit and poise in bringing together outrageous opposites with an artistic result that transcended, almost to annihilation, the things themselves. Samuel Johnson indicted the metaphysical poets for "the most heterogeneous ideas yoked by violence together"; but however violent the joining, sacred and profane love, religion and the sciences, eternity and death, everyday life and life's most exquisite moments all survived the clash intact and could even work together amicably in poetry, delivering conventional validations of themselves. Plath wore herself out on such contradictions to the extent that, for relief, she began treating them as mere jokes with her special blend of insouciance and determination, and communicating that the resulting cosmic comedy *was* the point, the joy, the freedom, and the redemption. This, I believe, proved to be her most vital breakthrough.

Plath's poems presaged Monty Python, and especially Terry Gilliam's animations, which are a comic and populist counterpart to all the schools of painting that had distanced themselves from the old rules of physical veracity. Gilliam presents mishmashes of mutilated sanctities, but they have their own mesmerizing logic: the predatory baby carriage, the pillar of society sprouting flowers from his head; the mock fairy tale "The Prince and the Black Spot" and the mock commercial "Purchase a Past," with their images of pullulating things that fill the frame and overwhelm a town and a home, respectively. Plath's "Mushrooms" has that same kind of merry fertile apocalypse as its story.

"Mushrooms" is syllabic (repeating numbers of syllables line by line rather than metrical patterns), and superficially like Marianne Moore's poetry that observes nature. Every line in these eleven three-line stanzas is five syllables long; and, to emphasize the regimentation, there are Moore-like harsh enjambments, lines ending in "very," "on," "We," and "are." But Plath answers Moore's intellectualism with heady literary sport. The form of "Mushrooms" clearly follows the content about the ironies of vulnerable things' adaptability. In nature, mushrooms burgeon in arbitrary-looking clusters in herbage, around the roots of trees, or in rotting material, but in civilized settings, they may fill crevices in hard man-made material with their own appearance of a disciplined invasion. Plath mentions paving, and I picture the cracks in a sidewalk and the spaces between paving stones, in which mushrooms would grow in long lines. By this time, Plath was used to England's penetrating damp, which helps mold and fungus spring up opportunistically in places where they are seldom seen in North America.

There are word-painting repetitions of words and phrases—"very," "us," "we," "So many of us!"—and of words of the same form: "earless," "eyeless," and "voiceless." Grammatical and syntactical elements also reproduce themselves in close quarters. There are six adverbs—five ending in y—in the six-word first stanza. In the third stanza there is parataxis, clauses in parallel without conjunctions where these would be expected: "Nobody sees us, / Stops us, betrays us": "or" is done without, as the mushrooms do without all but evanescently minimal food. The poem babbles with enthusiasm, it verbally bubbles, as the mushrooms bubble physically. But their loquacity is a thorough irony, as in reality nothing alive is more insensate than them. (Plants are far more mobile and reactive than fungi.) But *these* mushrooms in the end actually reveal themselves as intending a megalomaniac ambush of the world.

Someone could write a PhD thesis in an effort to do full justice to the sonic, imagistic, and allusory games in the poem. The second stanza embeds heavy o-sounds—notice also the internal near-rhyme

of "toes" and "noses," and compare "fists" and "insist,"
and "hammers" and "rams" a few lines down—where
the mushrooms are depicted as earthbound bodies,
then puffs out a-sounds as they emerge, breathe, and
(it's implied) find themselves with minds and the ambi-
tion to rise, a ridiculous ambition for this class of the
world's life, but only when you discount their per-
sistent energy:

> Our toes, our noses
> Take hold on the loam,
> Acquire the air.

With this transmigration of vowel sounds, Plath
delivers a cheeky new version of ancient physics and
cosmology and the role human thinkers and striv-
ers claimed in them. Earth and water are lower and
heavier, air and fire higher and lighter, and associated
with the highest, reigning divinity. Take a wild guess
where the upper-class, male philosopher or poet placed
his essential being, and where he placed animals' and
women's. But in Plath, mere mushrooms, by their sheer
determination, first master—"take hold on"—their
own element and then instantly annex the atmosphere:
"acquire" is the kind of word an aristocrat would use
for buying more land. Go ahead, underestimate mush-
rooms: that would be fun.

The message of activity and assertion is punched
home elsewhere by the clever use of juxtaposed words

with -ing endings. In another context, "bedding" and "paving" could be adjectives or participles indicating movement, but here they are mere static nouns, the resistant materials the mushrooms get through by their "heaving," a vigorous verb. The poem's other words with -ing endings are "nothing," the insubstantial food on which these creatures live, and "morning," the dawn of their victory. Plath had rehearsed such effects over many years. Long before, she had experimented with metaphoric meanings of the parts of speech: the poem "Verbal Calisthenics" (the title suggests the sheer rigor of her apprenticeship) begins with the lines "My love for you is more / Athletic than a verb."

The main rhetorical device of "Mushrooms" is the oxymoron, which serves the thematic joke of an obscurely developed yet in the end overwhelming power. These fungi are soft, colorless, voiceless, inconspicuous, and invisible in their movements; they are "Bland-mannered, asking / Little or nothing." But don't turn your back on them.

The mushrooms' contradictions are a drama and a story the poet tells as if from inside and outside at the same time. She observes them with a sort of amused disgust and dread, but she knows and feels what it is like to be them. They are fragile, helpless, food growing right out in the open, and without even roots to fix them in the ground. But they have a monstrous will like a supernatural force. It is a miracle like the loaves and fishes in reverse, because while the mushrooms are edi-

ble—or are they lying, and poisonous?—they are cer-
tainly not being eaten down to a few basketsful: just the
opposite. We are in solid biblical territory in reading
that the mushrooms are "meek" and will "inherit the
earth," as the meek in the Beatitudes will do after his-
tory ends in apocalypse. But the mushrooms are sneaky
creatures, in truth not meek at all, or their parting shot
would not be that their "foot's in the door," like a home
invader's.

Autobiographically, there are so many things the
poem *could* mean. Pretty obviously, the mushrooms
could be Plath herself, or the large and growing body
of her poetry, powerful by stealth. She was a female of
the mid-twentieth century, had grown up fatherless in
a household with little money to spare, and felt that
her talent was hopeless without relentless work, perfect
grades, plenty of fawning, and a sporty, cheerful, all-
American persona (with varsity sexual playmate added
after her first breakdown). She thrashed with frustra-
tion even as she rose. Both she and her brother worked
menial summertime jobs when they were young; but
he, smart and studious yet not a maniacal high-flyer
like her, had scholarships for the Phillips Exeter Acad-
emy and Harvard that substantially relieved him and
his family of worry and stress, whereas Plath went to
public schools and, in order to attend Smith, had to
add a painfully large portion of her mother's savings to
institutional funding and waitressing in her residence
throughout the academic term. Her brother had no

anxious backup plan for when the academic and pro-
fessional world might spit him out, no lowly but readily
marketable skill; Plath learned to type seventy words
a minute. As a wife, she kept house, worked as a sec-
retary when money ran low, and typed and submitted
her husband's poems. She would sit in silence through
literary parties while Hughes talked shop, though she
was building a portfolio of her own. But rhythmically,
like a machine, she pushed toward her ideal life and
work and against her doubts and despair. She would at
times rebel from harsh self-discipline and splash out on
sumptuous food and other luxuries; this would contrib-
ute to renewed panic about money; then she would go
back and work harder than before.

Another real-life resemblance that comes to mind in
reading "Mushrooms" is to Plath's mother Aurelia, the
quintessence of the household martyr. Disappointed
with her workaholic, rigid husband, she became a
suppressed, "submissive" (her word), but smoldering
wife, and in widowhood a whipsaw mother, now sick,
exhausted, bitter, and sanctimonious, now flattering
and complaisant against her judgment and indulgent
beyond her energy and means. For her daughter's thir-
teenth birthday, she copied out as a gift a poem about
a doll who exhausts her prating little owner with the
ceaseless grooming she requires. For her part, Sylvia
would write to her mother from Girl Scout summer
camp, from Yaddo, and from many places between and
beyond about how much and how well she was eat-

ing. These passages have tended to puzzle biographers, but a passage in *The Bell Jar* seems to explain them: the college-age protagonist is used to hearing at home the spiteful news of what food costs even as she eats it, so now in Manhattan she revels in gorging herself on rich meals in elite settings. In real life, Plath was taunting her mother with descriptions of the much better nour-ishment she could obtain for herself. Clearly, mother and daughter were deeply unable to stand each other, and at the same time worked like demons for each oth-er's shallow placation. And the intertwining was pro-longed beyond the grave. After Plath's death, Aurelia published a collection of the codependent letters home and insisted that her real daughter was cheerful, striv-ing, and adoring, a solid self that only powerful depres-sion managed to distort.

It could almost go without saying that "Mushrooms," written during Plath's first pregnancy, also reflects her deep ambivalence about fertility. A scene in *The Bell Jar* places the ambitious, fragile young protagonist, who is visiting a clinic for birth control, in a waiting room where she gawks at a mother and a baby, searching "for some clue to their mutual satisfaction." When she wrote this, Plath had already been a mother for many months; her fraught, touchy preoccupation with the role seems to have been a permanent thing. She waited much longer than most women of her generation to have children, agonized over time, finances, and her husband's attitude—but at one period claimed to be planning for several more, even pointing out to guests where the girls and boys would sleep. She proved by all accounts a pretty good mother (maybe too good in her control and organization), but her children were unquestionably part of her eventual catastrophe: she did not have the stores of health, energy, and optimism she needed for motherhood. The poem is prescient in showing fertility as literally, in terms of the Bible, apocalyptic; the mushrooms will take over a world that is ending; they are like one of the invasions or natural disasters destined to hasten its collapse.

Less personal potential meanings range freely through the poem as well. The mushrooms are the mass of unthinking, conforming people, repellent to the highly educated, self-assertive Plath. She was disgusted by fascism and the Red Scare and twentieth-century British and American imperial aggression, all four of which national majorities countenanced. From her teens, she had denigrated popular warmongering.

But all these are just my speculative impressions. There is no call to pin the poem down interpretively, and in fact trying to pin it down would spoil it; strain is as bad for a reader of poetry as for a poet. In any event, as an "exercise," perhaps one that Hughes had set to help her make the most of her time at Yaddo—her propensity was to work and fret herself into an artistic rut—the poem might evince concerns within easy and obvious reach to her, such as her fascination with the natural world. Plath was the daughter of a leading expert on bees and was old enough when he died for him to have shown off her knowledge of Latin taxonomical names to his colleagues. Some of her more famous poems were to be based on her own beekeeping. She also had a lifetime love of the sea and could be mesmerized by its fauna; and once she and Hughes owned a home, they gathered and sold wild daffodils from their grounds. It was in her character, and often fit her circumstances, to have small-scale, burgeoning nature on her mind. For his part, Hughes was a countryman and hunter in his bones, and at least as good a naturalist as she was.

But Plath and Hughes certainly did not see the world with rational, scientific eyes. They had a lively interest in the occult and were highly superstitious. They would invest the sight of an animal or a remark about one (a rabbit, say, with the potential to be trapped or run over by a car), or a dream about one (a talking fox, for instance), with meaning about the direction of their own lives; but of course they might be compelled over time to reinterpret. Their sense of even unlikely objects overflowing with mysterious, deceptive, or suddenly revelatory meaning enriched their poetry no end.

For Plath, this is particularly evident in her object poems. Not a thing is too bland, too trivial, too pretty, or too ugly—or too often used in poetry—to be alive and sentient and in some unheard-of but compelling relationship to the speaker. She is plainly off her imaginative head, making it all up as she goes along. Flowers are enemies, attacking the exhausted and inert speaker with their stimulating color and insisting on her responsiveness, and on a return to all the obligations now on hold ("Tulips"); or flowers taunt her with the drugs of oblivion that they withhold ("Poppies in July"). An elm tree is both a prophet who "know[s] the bottom" and speaks mockingly to the poet about her delusions, and a victim whose fate merges with hers ("Elm"). A cut finger during onion peeling is a scalped head, the symbol of all conflict and a harbinger of death ("Cut"). The moon in several poems is barren, yet a mother, yet an indifferent witness, yet hostile, but only because the universe is crazily intermeshed and dynamic: birth is tangled in death, love in withdrawal, beauty in the grotesque. It is not that way only theoretically, but as unmitigated and inescapable experience. "The blood jet is poetry, / There is no stopping it"—this is from a poem called, with shattering irony, "Kindness."

But Plath poems, whatever their more conventional influences and subject matter, are disproportionately about writing poetry. That is the message of their intricate and self-conscious forms. And poetry was the main purpose of Plath's life, a purpose to which she dedicated herself with a fervor unusual even among great writers. I read in "Mushrooms" that, though Plath never enjoyed much power in society or in the economy, on paper she could create and destroy like a god, like Terry Gilliam raising lunatic icons and then beheading them, like an obscure, frustrated, self-frustrating young

woman dreaming of the release of an army of conquer-
ing little words into a million imaginations—and then
going ahead and releasing them.

You're

JANUARY/FEBRUARY 1960

Clownlike, happiest on your hands,
Feet to the stars, and moon-skulled,
Gilled like a fish. A common-sense
Thumbs-down on the dodo's mode.
Wrapped up in yourself like a spool,
Trawling your dark as owls do.
Mute as a turnip from the Fourth
Of July to All Fools' Day,
O high-riser, my little loaf.

Vague as fog and looked for like mail,
Farther off than Australia.
Bent-backed Atlas, our traveled prawn.
Snug as a bud and at home
Like a sprat in a pickle jug.
A creel of eels, all ripples.
Jumpy as a Mexican bean.
Right, like a well-done sum.
A clean slate, with your own face on.

"**Y**OU'RE" is an ingenious ballooning of the old "What am I?" riddle. Instead of ending with the question "What am I?" the poem begins the answer in the one-word title, and then lists wildly fanciful, contrasting, in many cases weird and foreboding predicates to the title's subject. In these predicates, the pregnant woman snatches at identifications and descriptions of what she can sometimes feel but cannot reach with any of her other senses, and what may, when all is said and done, be marked for oblivion. Plath was an inveterate worrier, often dreading that she and her situation were not normal enough to afford her even the ordinary privileges of adulthood; and she would in fact miscarry one of her pregnancies after her husband assaulted her. But in "You're," a buoyant defiance of peril prevails. Questions unanswerable by science or culture or metaphysics are answered by poetry, her own very original poetry.

The traditional riddle is upended for fun like the clownlike fetus playing post-quickening tricks, and the reader is sent chasing after a whole flock of ungraspable, transmogrifying beings. The (presumably) human face at the end of the poem is paired with a slate, as if the representations only take on another category of slipperiness. The closest thing to the child's solid self will be what comes with the "well-done sum," or arithmetic problem solved: the artifact that is the smart, docile student. And that is years away, a dream and a possibility. Plath is treating her pregnancy, her

impending motherhood, her child-to-be the way she
treated her own process of literary composition—a
process that is pretty clearly illustrated in the poem: she
feverishly assembled impressions, whims, memories,
rhetorical and poetic strategies, and worked them over
in detail, but also made long imaginative leaps—with
everything aimed toward an idealized completeness.
Those dynamics can be seen across as well as within
poems. In March 1959, when she only believed that
she was pregnant, she wrote a poem eventually pub-
lished under the title "Metaphors," which depicts the
speaker as a hugely pregnant "riddle in nine syllables"
(the line length) and toys with a variety of images for
herself and the fetus, including bread dough rising, as
in "You're." A planned pregnancy is an excellent met-
aphor for a poetic career in that you need imaginative
propulsion just to start one, but over time you need
sheer patience and endurance.

Very likely stimulated by the reality of pregnancy,
"You're" is twice as long as and considerably more lively
than "Metaphors." The later poem is a tour de force of
metaphors, a witty boast that impending motherhood
has in no way diminished this woman's powers of mind
(the threat that Plath was used to hearing from mid-
century misogynists). The fetus as metaphor is itself a
poet's special pun. Metaphor means literally the thing
"carried with" or "carried over"; metaphor imposes a
far-fetched (sorry) meaning. A fetus is carried passive

in the mother's body, usually quite carefully and to short distances; but this fetus adventurously ranges the natural and cultural world at the same time.

For the reader picturing the mother's body, on the other hand, it could be the circus tent the clown performs in under the night sky, an aquarium or an ocean with the fish and the prawn in it, a drawer for the spool of thread, the night sky for the owls, the earth housing the turnip, a calendar of the pregnancy including the agricultural year and two holidays, a kitchen or oven for the loaf (cf. the old "bun in the oven"), the daylight sky in which vague fog is seen, the mailbox or house where the mail arrives and is taken in, a plant with its bud, the jug for the sprat, the basket for the eels, and the slate for the sum, which also offers its surface for a new portrait. The power of adding to humanity has expanded the pregnant woman into a world, into all kinds of places that harbor all kinds of things. Notable in this list are the means of civilizational creation. The poet-housewife's materials have taken on a life of their own, and she can anticipate the animated rewards of her sewing, marking dates, baking, sending out material for publication (Plath waited eagerly to hear editors' verdicts through the mail), storing up food, acquiring other food at a seafood market, and even, as an avocation, chalking the fetus into existence as an artwork (Plath was a gifted visual artist). It is less her biology that shelters and nurtures the baby than the sheer will to reach out to it and usher it into the world. Above all, this mother thinks, imagines, and incants the new life into existence; it is inseparable from her vocation as an author. This is, as far as I know, something brand new in literary history. Men were habitually pictured invoking new life by winning, supporting, protecting, celebrating, and (of course) impregnating women; women were supposed to be the passive, trusting nurturers.

Plath's at first strange-sounding take on pregnancy makes sense, first of all, in terms of her bold personal and intellectual history. For the obvious reason that literature was overwhelmingly male, the inscribed fetus had been close to nonexistent, and the baby since Homer and Greek tragedy little more than a creature who cooed, screamed, and made messes for years before becoming a full human being. Even once women could with propriety record something of the experiences of pregnancy and early motherhood, women authors were not such as could communicate these experiences with intimate credibility and sympathy. The majority of famous female authors were never even pregnant, and the experience of those who did conceive tended to be unedifying, to say the least. Plath is open to censure for allowing her ambitions, bad luck, and bad judgment to crash through her onto her children in the form of a breakdown and suicide; that is, she did not put her children first, as a mother is axiomatically supposed to do. But there is no comparison between Plath and, for example, the Russian poet Anna Akhmatova, who made touching poetic gestures toward her son but personally

treated him more or less as a disposable encumbrance—
though her own quite challenging life entreats us to cut
her some moral slack. Plath of course had it easier, but
she also really tried. She thought long and hard before
starting a family, and balanced her children's care with
determined ingenuity against the writing she would
not give up. When Frieda Rebecca, the child this poem
anticipates, was a toddler, she was taught to entertain
herself by drawing quietly within her mother's range of
vision. This reminds me of a later scene, with important
variations: Toni Morrison the editor writing fiction at
home with her small son close enough to throw up on
her manuscript (and also close enough that she knew
he was okay), but without letting him interrupt her
work. Plath's fate as a mother was worse in part because
her generation was less accommodating to professional
women whose marriages failed, but also because of
her self-consuming drive, which made even cleaning a
life-and-death contest in her mind: she did not have it
in her to take vomit—and everything else about chil-
dren—as it came. "You're," as a well-controlled, high-
test stunt, illustrates her dire—if stimulating—inner
strain. A writer like Toni Morrison could keep it real
with her children and mourn the too-true tragedies of
past motherhood without being psychically dragged
into them. Plath had to make motherhood something
else, something unusual, both in reality and on paper,
because she saw no yet-existing place in it where she
could rest.

The poem may adapt its structure from that of traditional riddles, but the restless ambivalence of its answers is no joke. As the daughter of a struggling widow who could not give her children all the time, material things, or experiences their age-mates enjoyed, and as a ravenously ambitious young woman in an era that strove to divide housewives and career women into separate camps and pit them against each other, Plath was leery of motherhood, and her leeriness did not disappear after childbirth. She rendered it perhaps most unforgettably in the black humor of *The Bell Jar*, written when her daughter was a toddler. A boyfriend smuggles the protagonist Esther into a hospital theater (what an apt word) to watch a woman laboring under a twilight-sleep drug that leaves her no role in the birth but to emit a high-pitched animal moan, and no awareness of her gory episiotomy or of her baby when it appears; Esther is outraged that the woman will not be able to remember her obvious agony, to be repeated at the end of the next pregnancy, which she will of course soon volunteer for.

But *The Bell Jar* episode also contains a heavy admixture of satire on the college girl's touchy mindset that produces this philippic against the manipulations of men. "You're," written when Plath was in her late twenties and in the midst of the pregnancy it describes, sounds indulgent and fascinated. It turns out to be true what they say, you feel differently later on, and when it's yours.

But the fetus in the poem only tangentially antici-
pates a baby, a tiny offspring of the same species. The
imagery of this creature is persistently not human,
though it appears to become so in the last line when
the fetus has its "own face on"—but is this face the
vital projection of a unique personality, or just a rough
chalk outline on the slate? In any case, the last line
leaps magically from the earlier exotic embodiments
to humanity, blanking out the late, distinctly human-
like stages of fetal development (the poem was written
quite late in Plath's pregnancy), the trauma of birth,
and the extreme dependence of infancy. But this struc-
ture seems right for how Plath continued to feel about
childbearing and motherhood: that it *should* be a sort of
organic magic. She could not, otherwise, have planned
to have several more babies when she was so consti-
tuted and situated as to buckle under two.

In any event, the scientific, expertly orchestrated,
rationalized, controlling American take on medicine
was something Plath loathed; the birth scene in *The Bell
Jar* parallels her memories of her first round of electro-
shock, which she experienced as a brutal effort to wipe
out her distress (and perhaps her self too) instead of
dealing with it. By January 1960, the earliest approxi-
mate date for the poem, she had deliberately returned
from a sojourn in America to Britain, with its surplus
hardships and risks, to give birth, and she was happy at
the prospect of a home birth with a midwife. The poem
likewise, though innovative in its form and content,

echoes ancient thinking: pregnancy and childbirth are just part of nature. Plath was no fool about nature, but nature, in her poetry, hardly has to seem easy to seem authoritative.

Her attitude, however, does not preclude ambivalence, irony, and even grim prophecy, according to the reader's own hindsight. The poem's speaker does nod to the beneficence of evolution: the human species with its opposable thumb can contrive and choose—"A common-sense / Thumbs-down"—not to go extinct, in "the dodo's mode." But the line, with its ho-ho long-o sounds and that comical bounce of a near-rhyme, combines two historical references that are wildly different but both disturbing: to the Roman amphitheater where the ruler, here standing for the mighty human race, bestowed life or death with a gesture of his hand; and the poor, stupid bird that had no defenses against colonial adventurism. This isn't a superiority from which the human race comes out looking noble.

And worse, this poem is about human *pregnancy*; in this realm, any smug speciesist thinking is likely to hit up against some sad ironies, at least in the mind of a biologist's daughter. Two critical human endowments, the large brain in the large skull that has to pass through the narrow birth canal, and the long period of dependency allowing for elaborate enculturation, charge our race's success disproportionately to females. Frieda's birth was easy and happy, and her care did not put unbearable strain on Plath's health, mood, or marriage. But Nicholas's birth less than two years later was agonizing and terrifying, and was added to new stresses in the interval between the pregnancies that included appendicitis and the miscarriage after a slap, or a beating, by Hughes. Plath had destroyed, or merely torn in two, writings of his in retaliation for his lateness, somewhere between fifteen minutes and two hours, in returning to babysit in order to free her for a moneymaking job; or, alternately, Plath had acted out of jealous suspicion of a female BBC functionary who was interested in Hughes's work. (Such differences in accounts leave me uncertain whether Plath or Hughes rewrote the relationship more thoroughly after it went bad; but Hughes had thirty-five years longer to do it, and more of his bad behavior is proven.) Motherhood turned into a crag from which Plath slid, bruised, torn, and struggling to right herself.

Most embodiments of the fetus in the poem are ridiculous or bizarre, and some might even be called grotesque. Not only are the post-quickening movements like a clown's acrobatics, but the clown's comical baldness slides into the skeletal baldness of the moon. The moon is almost never a friendly image in Plath: it is female, in line with its traditional association with the female monthly cycle, but it is generally a barren, hostile crone, a spirit of death.

Plath then applies her natural history expertise but overdoes it: the fetus at early stages does look somewhat like a fish (it is a dead, pickled sprat in the second stanza) or a shrimp, recapitulating early stages of human evolution; but, again, Plath was heavily pregnant when she wrote this. The poem thus embryolizes the almost fully formed fetus and backpedals from the looming birth. The baby is privileged, opposed to the extinct dodo, but it is no great feat to outdo a clownlike, notoriously stupid bird.

A spool, an owl ("Trawling your dark as owls do"— what a witchy, woeful-sounding swirl of sounds), and a turnip are hardly cuddly representations of human offspring. The owl is traditionally a bad omen. Any pregnancy may delude the family and turn out tragically, following up the explosive joy of its conception, "the Fourth / Of July," with April 1 or April Fools' Day—the interval being the approximate nine months of Plath's gestation. Frieda was in fact born on April Fools' Day, not exactly a nice thing to predict. Our ancestors' meaning for "giving birth to a fool" is not that the baby will turn out merely foolish, or like a Shakespearean clown who is wise under his cloak of nonsense, but that it will be the village idiot, like Christian Cantle in Thomas Hardy's *The Return of the Native*, whose mother accepts that there was never any hope for him, because he was born on the wrong date: "No moon, no man." Plath's use of the British name for the holiday, *All* Fools' Day, gives a further suggestion: human beings as a group are made fools of by our too-heavy investments in life and love. The last line of the stanza stands out for its tenderness and optimism. The belly rises, the delicious homemade loaf of the devoted housewife rises, and the baby will be tall and physically impressive and an achiever, a "high-riser" like both its parents.

But the beginning of the second stanza turns wistful. The mail was a fickle haunter of Plath's days; she had no insider status in any organization and was a perpetual petitioner, and the farther she got from her childhood in child-centered, prize-happy mid-century suburban America, the less often she was formally recognized for her brilliance. Rejection letters in response to her submissions and applications are a drumbeat of punishment in her journals. And she worried about motherhood too in terms of success and recognition, as if it were a performance.

Length of time becomes geographical extent in the next line. Australia is at the extreme southeast of the planet, and the Atlas of Greek and Roman mythology stands at the western end of the ancient known world. Frieda was conceived in New England and taken on a long and eventful car trip to the West Coast during her first few weeks in utero, then to England. In the poem, the tiny, prawnlike fetus migrates as if on its own as far as it is possible to go on earth, including to where the parents have never been. Hunched in a tiny C-shape, this creature is an ironic silhouette of the Titan Atlas eternally condemned to hold up the sky. A fetus is comprehensively upheld in a physical sense, but in other senses upholds the world: the mother's and family's and tribe's hopes, the whole human future.

Within a few more lines, the projections of the fetus move from still to animated. The bud is a tight, motionless part of a plant waiting for the season of opening. ("Snug as a bud and at home" is a paraprosdokian rhetorical figure—that is, the ending is unexpected: we expect the full "Snug as a bug in a rug" simile.) The sprat is dead and preserved, but the eels (a rhyming creel-full) appear to be alive, squirming in their basket, and the Mexican bean jumps around uncontained and uncontrolled, reminding me of the wry comments pregnant women make about the football or basketball game going on under their ribs. In this sense at least, the poem moves toward fetal development and birth.

Then all the chaotic images resolve in three things. First there is the "well-done sum," more an abstraction than an image, perhaps alluding to the logical give-and-take that does exist in nature and society, though there is no mathematical certainty about outcomes. Second, there is the "clean slate," a conventional metaphor that provides another calming moment: nothing has gone wrong yet; all may be right, like the sum. At the long-awaited moment of ecstatic resolution in *The Bell Jar*, Esther chants, "I am" over and over. In this poem, "sum" is a pun on the Latin word for "I am." Sometimes just to be alive is enough, and more than enough.

Finally, there is the face that, even if it is only an artifact, does belong to this human individual, as a representation of a unique body and soul. "Your own face on" is a lovely ending; it sounds like a mother proudly

and encouragingly equipping her child with an iden-
tity: there you go, this is for you, this is how you wear
it. In fact, the whole of "You're" can be seen as a ver-
bal version of the rituals investing a tiny child or even
an unborn one with its future. Parents draw or paint
a goofy portrait on the pregnant belly, tell the fetus
fanciful stories about itself, and when the baby appears
dress it up extravagantly and surround it with images
of the wider world—and some of these images may
be of creatures who are not cuddly at all, their ancient
purpose being apotropaic; that is, they are meant to
turn away evil by invoking it: a tiger, a bear, a dragon,
a shark. This poem feels apotropaic: a careful, fierce,
tender gift Plath made for her daughter.

The Babysitters

OCTOBER 29, 1961

It is ten years, now, since we rowed to Children's Island.
The sun flamed straight down that noon on the water
    off Marblehead.
That summer we wore black glasses to hide our eyes.
We were always crying, in our spare rooms, little put-
    upon sisters,
In the two huge, white, handsome houses in Swampscott.
When the sweetheart from England appeared, with
    her cream skin and Yardley cosmetics,
I had to sleep in the same room with the baby on a
    too-short cot,
And the seven-year-old wouldn't go out unless his
    jersey stripes
Matched the stripes of his socks.

O it was richness!—eleven rooms and a yacht
With a polished mahogany stair to let into the water
And a cabin boy who could decorate cakes in six-
    colored frosting.
But I didn't know how to cook, and babies depressed me.
Nights, I wrote in my diary spitefully, my fingers red

With triangular scorch marks from ironing tiny ruchings
    and puffed sleeves.
When the sporty wife and her doctor husband went on
    one of their cruises
They left me a borrowed maid named Ellen, 'for protection',
And a small Dalmatian.

In your house, the main house, you were better off.
You had a rose garden and a guest cottage and a model
    apothecary shop
And a cook and a maid, and knew about the key to the
    bourbon.
I remember you playing 'Ja Da' in a pink piqué dress
On the gameroom piano, when the 'big people' were out,
And the maid smoked and shot pool under a green-
    shaded lamp.
The cook had one wall eye and couldn't sleep, she was
    so nervous.
On trial, from Ireland, she burned batch after batch of
    cookies
Till she was fired.

O what has come over us, my sister!
On that day-off the two of us cried so hard to get
We lifted a sugared ham and a pineapple from the
    grownups' icebox
And rented an old green boat. I rowed. You read
Aloud, cross-legged on the stern seat, from the
    Generation of Vipers.

So we bobbed out to the island. It was deserted—
A gallery of creaking porches and still interiors,
Stopped and awful as a photograph of somebody laughing,
But ten years dead.

The bold gulls dove as if they owned it all.
We picked up sticks of driftwood and beat them off,
Then stepped down the steep beach shelf and into the
     water.
We kicked and talked. The thick salt kept us up.
I see us floating there yet, inseparable—two cork dolls.
What keyhole have we slipped through, what door has shut?
The shadows of the grasses inched round like hands of
     a clock,
And from our opposite continents we wave and call.
Everything has happened.

SOMETIMES A WORK that at first looks anomalous
can throw the author's achievement into helpful
perspective. Keats's delightful "A Song About Myself"
is about a poet at last defeated by his own whimsy: "So
he stood in his shoes /And he wonder'd." The larking
stanzas show Keats very much in control, in contrast
to his usual projection of transporting emotionality. In
"The Babysitters," Plath turned aside from the increas-
ingly grim, mystical subject matter of her poems, and
from the cold, swift, gripping style she was developing
in that genre, and presented a proselike narrative poem
that approaches conventional female literary wryness

and warmth. Two girls at the end of their teens conspire in quite a limited and harmless way against grown-up oppression; their victory is a moral and emotional more than a practical one, but it is important to them.

Not that Plath hadn't been in this territory long before, and not that she hadn't already learned richly from it. She was a frequent if rarely successful submitter of short stories to women's magazines, which liked to enshrine discrete, sympathetic, well-resolved dissidence. She was likely too submissive a submitter, too eager in offering the goody-goody, anything-you-want narrative confections that, in miniature, feature in her letters to her mother. But while still in college she confirmed her vocation as a writer by winning $500 in a *Mademoiselle* fiction contest for "Sunday at the Mintons'," a tale that culminates in a fey spinster's dull and pompous brother being overwhelmed by a wave and carried away—in her imagination. And at last, in early 1961, Plath began writing *The Bell Jar*: she pulled the rip cord of her prose fiction style and proceeded to glide through the sky in her confidence as a sardonic, truth-telling, but well-controlled performer.

"The Babysitters" draws on the lessons of that experience. Both the novel and the poem show some essentials of Plath's development more openly than her more typical poems do; in particular, they display her auto-biographical cunning. I use the word "cunning" in the archaic sense, as when the jeweler or forger of weapons did matchless work. As a writer with woeful disadvantages of circumstance and temperament—her sex, her family, her class, her nationality, and her swiveling self-hatred, rage, contempt, compulsive overwork followed by paralysis—Plath sporadically, and at last steadily, used retooled autobiography to make readers identify with her. Since she could not change her circumstances as much as she wished, or her temperament at all, she formed work that said, "I am the most poignant version of you, and I describe my experience the way you were just going to describe yours."

Most of us, like Miss Minton, Esther Greenwood, and the speaker in "The Babysitters," have experienced the repressed rages of dependency on obtuse, self-centered people: if nothing else, it is an ordinary part of childhood, youth, and enculturation. But Plath's depictions are minutely calibrated: not too angry and self-pitying (like her journals and some letters), and not false and pandering either (the way she wrote as a professional petitioner or the good little girl in relationships), but in a vivid and often ironic style; she presented awful things, which we are bound to care about, with a mixture of clinical precision and entertainment that make us trust her. This strategy underlies her late poetry too, but in that more imaginative, more mystical environment it is harder to see. Everywhere her cunning was honed, it could induce readers—women in particular—not just to watch, in retrospect, her flight toward self-annihilation with acute empathy from their safe place on the ground, but also to take on all sorts of wild identification with her: Plath seemed to represent and protect them personally, like a patron goddess, in their self-expression and other aspirations; some of them protected her memory and went to war against both her enemies in life and the enemies of her posthumous influence. The mood about her is calmer now that time has shrunk these overlapping camps. But the productive shock Plath delivers in her autobiographical wizardry still meets generation after generation.

In some ways "The Babysitters" is anomalous. Plath did not have ordinary attachments to other women; she had not reached out to a female friend with a poem since one written in 1945, which depicts two teenyboppers in a picturesque and adorable confab at Girl Scout camp. You couldn't make this stuff up, the greeting-card expressiveness that Plath was liable to stoop to, and against which she reacted with a vengeance. "The Babysitters" has its artificialities too, such as "wav[ing] and call[ing]" to a friend beyond the ocean, but I would not include the poem in this volume if I did not think that with it Plath works the magic that is characteristic of her artistic coming of age.

Autobiographical background is riveted to the poem, as it is to *The Bell Jar*. In 1951, two years before her attempted suicide and the start of her inpatient psychiatric treatment, Plath got a summer job through the Smith college vocational office. She and her friend Marcia Brown were to work for two families as nannies in mansions close by each other on the Massachu-

setts shore. The details of the poem are all verified in
Plath's letters and diaries, and it is interesting to see
that the poem not only selects fastidiously but softens.
Plath's job was not just enough to drive a girl to secret
tears and spiteful diary entries; it was a bait and switch,
advertised as childcare only, but actually entailing
cooking, cleaning, and laundry, plus secretarial work
for the physician head of the house, as well as the care
of three small children. It was not merely that Plath
couldn't cook: she was treated as if she had swindled
her employers by showing up without the mastery of
work they had not specified. She did not merely burn
her fingers ironing; she cut them repeatedly in the
kitchen in her distracted hurry with unfamiliar imple-
ments and hid the bleeding for which she feared being
blamed. The children not only depressed her; she
fantasized about killing them and privately penned
a spoof headline news story to that effect. They not
only had fussy clothes that the poem shows her iron-
ing, and not only was one of them a troublemaking
clothes snob; they shrieked and fought uncontrollably,
and their impositions went on at intervals throughout
the night. Their socialite mother was seldom around,
leaving them to the inexperienced "help," who was
apparently not authorized either to discipline them or
to call her in as a disciplinarian; when the mother *was*
around, it was less to pitch in than to stop her hireling
from sitting down for a break during the fourteen-hour
day. The yacht may have been luscious, but Plath was

not usually included in the posh outings. She was desperately angry, but quitting could have left her short of money for her next college year and blackballed for other jobs: her boss might avenge the defection with a crippling reference.

Nothing among literary reputations is more unfair than Plath as a hysterical poet. Those who have not read her, and those unfamiliar with the hard-nosed realism and strict anger management working women were and still are forced into, may smear her in this way on the basis of the subject matter for which she is best known: depression, marital breakdown, suicide. A moralist could comment on how much condemnation Plath earns for having sometimes lost control in life. (But such an expert might be better employed among the living.) Mere readers are met in Plath's poems with miracles of transformation: fury, hatred, violence, mutilation, and death are presented through cartoonish images, humorous language, and far-out metaphoric stagings—for example, a freak show for suicide in "Lady Lazarus." Utter exhaustion and emptiness are mediated by physical distance in scenes of natural beauty: the feeling that threatens to annihilate me is in the sky or in the roots of a tree; it is thus part of the way things are, and of ongoing life. "The Babysitters" takes what in reality had been an aggravation of Plath's already serious depression and exhaustion, and a revelation that adult life would bring routine mistreatment for a poor but brilliant female with literary ambitions, and makes it all bearable for us, not only bearable but charming.

The poem does this in part by adapting language from fairy tales and other children's literature. It begins by fronting the rowboat journey to Children's Island (cf. Neverland, the island where Peter Pan and his Lost Boys live), to which the "little put-upon sisters" (twin Cinderellas) will head at last in their escape from uncaring and oblivious adults. In realms of folklore, if the heroine can just get away, out of the witch's or monster's clutches, out of the dark forest or cruel household, all will be well. But her typical plight falls short of the worst adult horrors. Most fairy tale heroines are not tortured or married by force or even subjected to brutally unfair employment conditions but overlooked in favor of the undeserving or given comically impossible tasks, such as fetching water in a sieve, and then quickly saved from them.

The torments of the poem's speaker and her friend are almost as silly-sounding; they are also overdramatized through Plath's parodic take on her own late adolescent voice. The girls hide their red eyes with sunglasses, but there is no hint that anyone else cares how they look. As a mere matter of course, and with no outward rivalry or jealousy, the sweetheart from England displaces the nanny to the children's room; there the nanny merely suffers the farcical awkwardness of a bed too short for her. (I can picture the willowy Plath thrashing around in search of a position that

will allow her to sleep.) The nanny has the ridiculous
task of either convincing a six-year-old that his fashion
sense is too keen or meekly dressing him to his exact-
ing specifications, which will encourage him to no end
of further toying with his helpless lackey.

"And the seven-year-old wouldn't go out unless his
jersey stripes / Matched the stripes of his socks" is a
little jewel of Plath deadpan, like *The Bell Jar*'s "mirac-
ulous furpiece" (the union of a dime-store fake gold
chain and wholesale foxtails). It isn't just my training in
classical philology that gives me a sense of Plath's late
writings as exquisite artifacts. Since settling in Con-
necticut, I've learned a little about the antiques trade,
and have come to appreciate the genesis of furniture I
can't afford. In both words and wood, really fine work
is not only quickly recognizable; it also invites you to
turn the thing over, take the pieces apart if possible,
and examine the inward structure; even the oddities
and contrivances (the hidden supports for the legs,
an unusual wood used for the back or the bottoms of
drawers; the quiddities of vocabulary or word order)
strike you as the signs of a lively, stubborn skill. These
two lines in "The Babysitters" come from a person who,
with the help of exhaustive literary training, was echo-
ing her own youthful impression of a snippy seven-
year-old boy; at this stage of her vocation, the poet
could maneuver to achieve just the right tone.

One unusual thing about the lines is the repetition of
the word "stripes," which breaks a conventional rule of

modern English style. Why didn't Plath rearrange the rather awkward sentence to avoid the need to repeat a word? But the awkwardness draws attention to itself for good reasons. "Stripes" and then again "stripes" suggests a long, exasperating discussion with the boy. But the lines also tap into the ancient, deep spring of poetry, and resound with the heartbeat of aesthetics, repetition with variation: "*his* jersey stripes," and "the stripes *of his* socks" have a beat, but the elements alter to make the beat interesting, as with Plath's near-rhymes in tighter poems. And the sentence has wit, ending with the bathetic "socks" (rhymes with cocks and bollocks) instead of shoes or pants or a bathing suit: this wrangle is about *a child's socks,* which he shouldn't need at all during a summer on the beach. But Plath also pulls a little cultural fast one; when she wrote this poem, she was living in England and had a British audience, so she called the shirt a "jersey." She has enough rhetorical authority to get away with this with an American audience.

The poem's speaker, so carefully scripted, is (and the young Plath was) as enthralled with the mansion, the yacht, and the skilled servant decorating exquisite pastry as Apuleius's Psyche is with the enchanted palace, but the speaker is not the entitled protagonist of such a story and is not even any familiar protagonist type; but she is deeply real. She describes her own diary entries as spiteful; she sees her ambitious writer's fingers disfigured by ironing fancy make-work toddlers' dresses, and any personal satisfaction she will ever get is distant and vague. These people do not care, and will never care, that she thinks she is superior to them. (The son, in fact, who as a small child had demanded a matching ensemble to wear for playing outdoors, was interviewed as an adult and pronounced on Plath's shortcomings as an underling.) They treat her as a delinquent appliance, bringing in a real servant not to help but to keep an eye on her in their absence; a useless "small Dalmatian" is somehow part of the arrangement.

Through such astutely selected and presented autobiographical realities, Plath achieves a rare degree of personal sympathy in readers. In fact, she creates penetrating partisanship, even in people who know about her daunting complexities and her serious failings. I know that she was no Cinderella, that she fantasized when she should and could have been looking out for herself and repeatedly set herself up for situations like this. In this case, she had had a boyfriend drive her to Boston's North Shore for an excited preview of the compound, and she later wrote that she had "assumed" that only "occasional" surveillance of the children would interrupt her relaxing on the beach, swimming, and writing. Nevertheless, in rereading "The Babysitters," I was driven back once again to the magisterial Clark biography for more details about the summer job, and then I began to fume over the outrage of keeping this poor domestic worker on twenty-four-hour shifts; yes, and I recalled that my husband, when he was

a lawyer in private practice, had won hefty back pay
for a client from a socialite employer who did exactly
that to her. I did some online research and calculated
how far below the minimum wage of the time Plath's
pay was, and I remembered a doctor's sporty wife of
my own acquaintance, who asked me to teach her chil-
dren Latin for $2.50 an hour toward my college tuition,
explaining to me that this offer, though far below the
minimum wage, was fair and nonnegotiable because
this wouldn't be teaching of any kind: I would just be
correcting the children's work. I was too polite to ask
what would happen if I held her to that and refused
to explain my corrections or go over the reasoning
behind them. Now, forty years after that encounter, I
sat in my office smoldering about my own wrongs and
Plath's together. But this is just a sign of her particu-
lar genius. She wrote so as to seem to know a reader's
number, whatever it happens to be.

The lament over the job is distinct in the first two
stanzas. At "In your house, the main house, you were
better off," both mood and story line change. The lan-
guage of children's literature continues, but the house
of oppression is left behind, and a children's paradise
is suggested by the rose garden, the model apothecary
shop, the pink piqué dress, the game room, and the
"'big people'" who are away; and the servants remind
me of protagonists' adult confederates in children's lit-
erature: they are often raffish, marginal people, the sort
who have time for children and an offbeat charm. But

the sneaked bourbon, the smoking, pool-playing maid, and the wall-eyed cook too disturbed to bake cookies, who is fired from what may be her last-chance job, are grimly comic adult elements crowding in. And clearly, the only person who cares what the speaker is going through, the only one who shares any of her frustrations and goes out on a limb with her to make a small part of their summer a chance for real relaxation and conversation, is her friend. In this too, the spoof of the fairy tale is sympathetic and believable. There is no Prince Charming to come to the rescue, but you do know in a pinch who your friends are.

In the next stanza, there is another change, and a greater one. The climactic escape by water runs aground on a very adult sense of emptiness and disillusionment. This is not *Huckleberry Finn*, in which a naïve escape voyage is led to a happy ending by a protective author. The two girls do beg for the outing with tears, like children, and they raid the "grownups' icebox" for a whole ham and pineapple, which would make for messy and excessive eating; they are not thinking, only impulsively grabbing and running; Mark Twain would certainly bail them out.

Plath doesn't. The mood is much more subdued during their journey, and unrelieved on their arrival. The friend sits cross-legged like a child but reads aloud from quite a nasty adult book, *Generation of Vipers* by Philip Wylie, best known for its indictment of the lazy, martini-swigging, bullying American Mom. Does this figure stand for the present tyranny they endure, or for the role they may play themselves when they are married women with families? The girls' destination, Children's Island, off the town of Marblehead, has a dismal history: an inoculation hospital burned down by locals, a defunct sanitarium, a resort that languished for lack of water. The YMCA camp that was to anchor the place as a recreation center was not started until 1955, and the only signs of civilization that the young women find are deserted, end-of-season vacation homes, "Stopped and awful as a photograph of somebody laughing, / But ten years dead."

They have to fight off aggressive gulls just to command the beach and take a dip. What they do during it—"We kicked and talked" (there is no hint about what), buoyed by the "thick salt"—is the climax of the poem. The friendship finds time and privacy for itself only in this bleak and distant place. Yet the poet's memory of the "two cork dolls" sends her into the closest thing to an expression of pure affection that she is capable of in her literary maturity. She now writes almost as if the geographical separation of herself and her friend and the passage of time are a sort of cosmic wrong, and as if the friends long to come together again and catch up on their news of "everything."

But distance has craftily mitigated human feeling from the first lines of the poem: "It is ten years, now, since we rowed to Children's Island. / The sun flamed straight down that noon on the water off Marblehead":

a decade's time, the stretch of ocean water, the height
of the sun at midday—as the scene is set, the overcom-
ing of distance is achieved only by a boat moving by
slow human power, and the sun with its searing heat:
hardly comforting images. By the end of the poem, the
distance becomes a whole ocean, and intimacy is cut
off not only by the immense water, but also by the mas-
sif of adult independence and chosen personal history,
the thing the speaker was frantic for to protect herself,
as her creator's journal witnesses. Whatever door this
is, it was shut by her consent.

The sense of deflation is reinforced by the poem's
physical structure; each stanza is convex, starting with
moderately short line, including at least one notably
longer one, and ending with a quite short one, at least
twice as short as the one immediately before it, but in
most cases shorter than that: the stanzas end in six, four,
four, four, and at last three words. In those lines are the
annoying socks, the small Dalmatian, the fired cook,
the person long dead, and "Everything has happened."
Since the Sapphic stanza (three lines of eleven sylla-
bles, then a five-syllable line) dating from the seventh
or sixth century BCE, this sort of truncation has been
used to great effect, seeming to signal that words fail
the poet at the end of each unit of thought or memory:
emotion is too strong, an impression too powerful. The
most famous such poem of antiquity is one of Sappho
in which the speaker has a terrible seizure of jealousy

but endures it in silence; the final words translate as
"I seem to be almost dying." The final line of Plath's
poem, "Everything has happened," is more portentous
than it would be if the stanza had another shape. Is
the line thematically parallel to the other last lines, in
which stupid and awful things happen, or is it in coun-
terpoint, suggesting a better adult world? Or can we
even guess? Are the two friends now so far separated
in their feelings and experiences that the "Everything"
is only a wall of mystery? In any case, it is an arresting
line: sweeping, teasing, tautological.

In a famous simile in the *Iliad*, blood from a wound
of the warrior Menelaus (the cuckold for whose sake
the Trojan War is happening, and a third-rate fighter
himself) is likened to red dye on an ivory bridle orna-
ment, the work of a foreign woman and the envy of
horsemen—but the king stores it safe in his chamber
for his own delight and future use. Homer's combined
images of a fecklessly acquired wound and intelligent
craftsmanship are nicely applicable to his own work.
Great poetry makes an exquisite, lasting treasure out of
passing pain and shortcoming, with deliberated beauty
intervening in what is brutal, sordid, ordinary, and self-
centered to create a breathtaking balance and a heart-
opening sense of the human condition. As a woman
poet, Plath does this in her own terms, making the
story of a botched late-adolescent summer of domes-
tic work an illustration not only of the unbreachable

gaps between people and the difficulties in maintaining relationships, but also of the energizing and productive longings and the inviting blank pages that may rise from those very limitations.

The Applicant

OCTOBER 11, 1962

First, are you our sort of a person?
Do you wear
A glass eye, false teeth or a crutch,
A brace or a hook,
Rubber breasts or a rubber crotch,

Stitches to show something's missing? No, no? Then
How can we give you a thing?
Stop crying.
Open your hand.
Empty? Empty. Here is a hand

To fill it and willing
To bring teacups and roll away headaches
And do whatever you tell it.
Will you marry it?
It is guaranteed

To thumb shut your eyes at the end
And dissolve of sorrow.
We make new stock from the salt.
I notice you are stark naked.
How about this suit——

Black and stiff, but not a bad fit.
Will you marry it?
It is waterproof, shatterproof, proof
Against fire and bombs through the roof.
Believe me, they'll bury you in it.

Now your head, excuse me, is empty.
I have the ticket for that.
Come here, sweetie, out of the closet.
Well, what do you think of *that*?
Naked as paper to start

But in twenty-five years she'll be silver,
In fifty, gold.
A living doll, everywhere you look.
It can sew, it can cook,
It can talk, talk, talk.

It works, there is nothing wrong with it.
You have a hole, it's a poultice.
You have an eye, it's an image.
My boy, it's your last resort.
Will you marry it, marry it, marry it.

I N SEPTEMBER 1953, at the age of twenty, Sylvia Plath
entered the McLean private mental hospital outside
Boston and began psychotherapy to address the anxi-
ety and depression that had caused a suicide attempt
a few weeks before. This was in an era when psycho-
analysis was still on the rise. In the eyes of the cultural

elite to which she yearned to belong, the movement paralleled literary modernism as an influential new way to understand alienation and psychic distress. The poet Robert Lowell was one of several famous McLean patients, treated there with some version of the "talking cure," and both he and Plath wrote in the "confessionalist" strain about the experience.

By most accounts, the success of Plath's own talking cure was mixed. Her therapist Ruth Beuscher (also called Barnhouse) did become the closest thing to a lasting confidante she ever had; the two corresponded until a few days before Plath's death—but more as friends than as doctor and patient. Plath (in my opinion) should have taken Beuscher's hard-nosed advice when her relationship with her husband turned irretrievably ugly (see Heather Clark's meticulous account of the breakup): she should have taken the lead in divorce proceedings and put him at every kind of distance.

Plath, however, never eager to take practical and realistic account of her emotional life, was apt to fixate instead on abstractions like the occult, and to be fascinated by psychoanalysis as a set of theories. She wrote her college senior thesis on the use of the double in two of Dostoyevsky's novels, showing how one character's repressed personality traits were inexorably expressed in another character. In her own poetry, she made constant use of the symbolic principle, that we can sometimes understand events better through narratives and images that have no obvious or direct relation to them.

During the period when her genius flowered, therefore, Plath took a preoccupying interest in *feelings and ideas about* the mind, at the cost of actions such as getting her painful partner out of her life for good. Paradoxically, the chance for this very concentration, which allowed her at last to pursue in earnest her dream of becoming a great writer, came about through the everyday, material circumstances of the marriage's breakdown. Her previous big literary growth spurts had come when she was left more or less alone: at Yaddo, where she was fed, housed, and given a private workspace; and in the studio of friends for entire mornings as she wrote *The Bell Jar,* working in a genre in which she had no mentors or overseers. In her final months, she felt (and to a great extent, was) abandoned by her husband. She lived first in the couple's Devon home and then in her own London flat; she was tied down by childcare but found that if she woke very early in the morning, she had hours to herself for writing. As a dutiful wife, she had been answerable to her husband's schedule, to say nothing of his influence on her thoughts, feelings, and work. Now she had an open-ended opportunity to explore language and the psyche on her own.

And she sometimes came to revolutionary conclusions. For women, the psychotherapeutic ethic stressed adjustments to a subordinate life. A woman was "healthy" if she accepted servile and objectified roles, "neurotic" if she resisted them. She even had to pretend that penetrative sex alone, with no attention to her clitoris, gave her an orgasm. Plath, with her strong sex drive, left therapy in the sanctioned clown costume of a platinum-blond movie vamp, pledged to presenting men with their shallowest fantasies and getting whatever they deigned to give her in return. No wonder that in her solitude near the end of her life, the psychoanalytical landscape seemed to her more and more of a black-humor phantasmagoria. In "Daddy," the Electra complex turns into a grotesquerie of historical proportions, complained of in childish rhymes yet invoking the Holocaust. In "The Applicant," the domestic-helpmeet-paradise take on marriage, for which psychotherapy provided a cover of expertise that Madison Avenue seized on, becomes an emporium for unresisted mutilations of the self. This is shown with excoriating irony. The usual persona of the psychotherapist in the mid-century popular media was that of a grave, wise, humane confessor-priest and healer, who makes the patient whole again, body and soul, and opens the way to freedom and fulfillment. In this poem, the pseudotherapist is a huckster Dr. Frankenstein who knows from the beginning what he is doing—pushing an entire alien, mutilated life onto a susceptible person (two of them, if the doll-woman still counts as a person)—and does not either hesitate or accept hesitation. Salesmanship and phony psychic healing, as Betty Friedan documented in *The Feminine Mystique*, can be merged into a single, poisonous entity: it was in fact a concerted project of advertisers, aided by the Institute for Motivational Research, to tell women in the voice of beneficent authority that buying the latest cake mix or floor wax would cure their feelings of purposelessness and alienation.

In the poem, however, Plath does not attack psychic manipulation and exploitation as straightforward outside forces. She meditates on passivity, complicity, ambivalence; she implies pity for the male husband-to-be figure, though her own husband had by this time left her for another woman, complaining that she had trapped him in her controlling domesticity and greed; and these attitudes hover over "The Applicant" like a miasma that paralyzes the soul.

Besides her experience of psychotherapy and her abiding interest in the field, Plath had had an inside view of the machine of commercialism. She held a college internship at *Mademoiselle* during June 1953. A hinge scene in *The Bell Jar*, which autobiographically depicts that job as the immediate impetus for her first suicidal breakdown, takes place when the whole class of young female interns are having their photos taken to appear in the magazine. As Plath was, the protagonist Esther is a monthlong guest and potential recruit of the fashion, beauty, and homemaking hype industry, has contracted ptomaine from a lunch prepared in the magazine's model kitchen, and has been assaulted by a sadist at an outlying party. At last, instead of keeping her body and self cheerfully on the promotional conveyor belt, Esther does as Plath did: she breaks down in tears while posing for a photo summing herself up with a single object; for her this is a rose grabbed from a bouquet to signify that she wants to be a poet. In the setting of the hypercompetitive magazine office, there is no possibility of acknowledging anyone as a suffering human being in need of comfort—though the whole pretext of the magazine is the fulfilment of personal needs. Instead, the room empties out except for Esther, and when she has calmed down and begun to fix her makeup, the editor breezes back with a pile of fiction submissions to review, saying they will "amuse" the young woman. Esther gamely digs in and fantasizes that in the near future she will surprise the editor with the brilliance of her own pseudonymous submission. This is of course a satire on a young, naïve, ambitious American woman's gullibility: Esther tries to believe she can be there and yet not there in the fast lane, outsmarting it and playing it for what she wants most. In the first part of the novel, she is charmed by the illusion that the free samples of merchandise, showy outings, and hip people represent a world opening up for her enjoyment and reward; but nevertheless, her deeper awareness that this is all just ruthless salesmanship does not budge. Such an awareness made a major contribution to the young Plath's despair and withdrawal; the photo of her that *Mademoiselle* ran shows her grinning

too widely, thin, sunken-eyed, half-hunched in the cor-
ner of a sofa, dangling the rose almost straight down;
a plate of exotic-looking fruit is sitting in the center
of the sofa, where she should sit. And as it turned out,
Plath continued to struggle, many years later, from the
lack of advantages she might have secured by being
"our sort of a person" to the women's magazine hierar-
chy, and to all the powerful hawkers of images and lies
she could reach.

Even as a very young woman, Plath could be quite
frank to herself about the transactional world and her
low position in it. A college-era journal entry shows
her downcast after spending a month's pay from a
news office job on a pink-lined raincoat. She resents
the salesgirl's smiling obliviousness to her poverty
and to how much work goes into her acquisition of a
few attractive things. Plath satirizes the encounter in
The Bell Jar. Esther asks a salesgirl whether a raincoat
is water-repellent and is lectured that no raincoat "is
ever water-*repellent*. It's showerproofed." Esther buys
it, and rain seeps through it as she visits her father's
grave. Except for a few generous grants (a Fulbright
scholarship was most important), Plath's economic and
vocational life never stopped being like this, a sancti-
monious shortchanging to which she was a knowing
but willing—or just helpless?—party. The figure in
"The Applicant" does not protest against the pitch
that the suit he needs in order not to be "stark naked"
is "waterproof, shatterproof, proof / Against fire and

bombs through the roof"—a typical Plath singsong of irony, of satire, of I'm-out-of-here bitterness.

But in the poem Plath is also exploring a deeper problem, the commercialization of private thoughts, emotions, and relationships. She is pillorying psychotherapeutic authority that claims to patch up intimately troubled situations with talk, in what is at bottom a commercial transaction. She was a veteran of for-profit American medicine; her mother had paid through the nose for primitive electroshock therapy for her, which was done without anesthetic, and which broke some patients' backs with the violence of the convulsions. Plath later secured treatment at McLean Hospital with its literary and Brahmin patina; a wealthy patron sprang for her stay. The main thing at issue in "The Applicant," help touted for becoming whole, recalls psychotherapy as a consumer product offered years before to the poet as a remedy for her suicidal desperation, in which her unhealthy relationship with her mother was implicated. In *The Bell Jar*, the healing epiphany is supposed to come when Esther, encouraged and affirmed by the therapist, manages simply to say that she hates her mother. The talking cure was meant to have lasting efficacy, but for Plath the talk never produced a fully honest, sustainable relationship with anyone—not others, and not herself—and by the time she wrote this poem, Plath was coming unstuck again.

And now the main partner in Plath's psychic entanglements was a husband no longer sold on the marriage

—I use the word "sold" deliberately, as the poem conveys his attitude in retail terms. From sometime before the birth of the couple's second child, Hughes began to feel trapped by his ambitious, acquisitive American wife, and he was to memorialize this in a work entitled *Difficulties of a Bridegroom,* which was broadcast on the BBC. The wife in this drama manifests as a rabbit he needs to run over, because she is also the witch bride with body parts made up of loathsome vermin, the bride who insists on selling his freedom for luxurious domesticity.

But "The Applicant," blossoming in this carpet-bombed landscape, demonstrates the unique freeing power that writing gave to Plath. She is breathtakingly imaginative and emotionally open as she applies the psychological idea of the double to herself and her vanishing partner. Her grievances against Hughes are turned upside down, or perhaps inside out. She inserts herself—as when *she* faced powerful commercial authority and was reduced to tears because she had nothing to offer but her natural (here, "stark naked") self—into an at first sexually ambiguous figure. "Rubber breasts" as well as other manufactured, replacement body parts would do to recommend this person, and the requisite genitals are only a vague "crotch." (The Thalidomide scandal had come to a head in 1961; thousands of babies were born with stunted or missing limbs and the need for prostheses due to the exuberant marketing of a palliative drug that had not

had adequate testing. Plath wrote the poem "Thalido-
mide" a few weeks after "The Applicant.") The reader
does not know that the person is male until a blood-
less, completely objectified female mate is pitched to
him. The initial ambiguity in a matter as important as
which sex a figure belongs to makes for a blurring of
the boundaries between the couple that the poem will
use to unfold sensitive and disturbing questions. Who
is being exploited more in the end, who is more pas-
sive or complicit, who has real choices, who will have
more to complain about when the whole saga is over?
Who is whose double, foisting off onto the other an
unwanted, repellent personality? Certainly the disem-
bodied voice of authority cannot plausibly bear all the
responsibility here.

The wordless, weeping person at first seems to be at
an interview—and interviewing was something Plath
had much more experience of than Hughes: she was
the one who dressed up, perched on chairs, and pre-
sented herself for the establishment's inspection, hop-
ing for life-changing favors. In any event, the applicant
of the poem cannot be considered for whatever he is
seeking—a job, it soon emerges—because he is unim-
paired. This establishment does not want him unless
he is mutilated (that is, "our sort of a person") and in
need of the job to buy medical appliances. "How can
we give you a thing?" is double-talk for a ridiculously
circular con. Nothing is free here, and the commerce is
in phony body parts to fill in for the real ones, after the

company steals these away or destroys them. In a grotesque form, the old advertising ploy of creating a need and at the same time offering to fill it is on display here: only now a life's vocation is toyed with in this way.

What whole, self-respecting person would take the deal as presented? But the interviewer has a strategy against stubbornness: to reject the man for his independence and integrity, so that he stands alone crying. He is indeed single, and so no proper member of society. He is then offered, as a remedy for his alleged utter need—shown by his empty hand—a mate who is at first represented by another hand, presumably detached and as empty as his own. The hand is touted as a tireless, all-purpose servant. But a hand, as in "to give one's hand," is of course a metonymy for marriage; he is really being offered not a servant but a wife.

In either case, the come-on is a con: the hand is a heartless, brainless tool, good only to make the motions of serving tea and stroking a forehead, and to "thumb" a corpse's eyes shut as a book or catalog is thumbed, a motion of casual perusal. Though the hand is imputed "sorrow" and certified to weep at the loss of its owner ("dissolve of sorrow"), the lies are blatant: this is an object designed to be recycled and sold to someone else: "We make new stock from the salt."

For the addressee's lifetime, however, this dubious but required article is nonreturnable and not disposable: he has to marry it, to make a traditional, permanent bond with it. A few years earlier, laid up with a

bad cold and (as usual) obsessing about her marriage,
Plath recorded in her journal how she had been read-
ing American women's magazines with their catalogs
of marital misery. A crescendo of her disgust comes at
the "Can This Marriage Be Saved?" feature of the *Ladies'
Home Journal*, where the authority of psychology pre-
sides over the crises:

> . . . — adultery, love affairs, childless women,
> incommunicative & sullen couples — "Can this
> marriage be saved?" The psychologist asks of
> two selfish, stupid, incompatible people who
> were idiots to marry in the first place. It came
> over me with a slow wonder that all these arti-
> cles & stories are based on the idea that passion-
> ate & spiritual love is the only thing on earth
> worth having & that it is next to impossible to
> find and even harder to keep, once caught.

Plath's instincts were in the right direction. The per-
fectly fulfilling marriage was a manipulative fantasy
dangled in front of a trusting public—as a huckster
dangles it in front of the silent man in "The Appli-
cant." And this was done for a reason. The mid-century
American economy, turned mainly to civilian purposes
after the all-out war effort that had grown it to a size
never seen before, had an unlimited appetite: there
was no privacy of mind or body or relationship, and
no sanctity of the culture, that it did not lick or gnaw

at, feeling for what it might extract, and announcing its hunger as beneficence.

The cost of the appliance-hand isn't revealed up front, for a reason obvious to the reader: the price would scare the daylights out of the poor customer—if he had undisturbed access to his own feelings. What he is expected to buy along with the hand has no sticker price either: a magical business suit. In this place, you pay through the nose in order to slave your life away and maintain your prosthesis, your alleged helpmeet. The suit is also touted as meeting all needs, not in the realm of care but of protection. Plath, a pacifist Unitarian in her youth, remained an advocate of disarmament and marched in a mass protest in London, taking her newborn daughter along. As I read "proof / Against fire and bombs through the roof," the voice of the poem is like the military-industrial complex, talking up useless or even destructive technology as an assurance against destruction.

But before the addressee can respond (if he is going to), there is another upsell, this one pledged to fill his empty *head*, his whole awareness and purpose, not just the physical and emotional needs signified by his empty hand. It is an obedient, pretty sort of animated mannequin stored in a closet until summoned out. It is naked like the customer, and for now worth no more than the paper gift customary on the first wedding anniversary, but the salesman talks up its rising value as if this is inherent and independent of the owner's efforts, like the value of a premium stock. But of course this man will be only the overburdened caretaker of this piece of property: he will have to buy it the clothes and jewelry that broadcast its value—and the jewelry will become costlier as the years and anniversaries wear on. Yes, it can sew—but not the suit: he has to buy that standard and ready-made. It can cook, but that will not make up for its brainless "talk, talk, talk": its propensity for that takes up a whole line.

By this time in their lives, the Plath-Hugheses had gone from bohemian to bourgeois. Hughes had recognition and reliable income through the literary establishment. Plath had been catching up but had urged him in the meantime to make the TV appearances he despised in order to earn more money. They had bought a substantial property, renovated and cultivated it, acquired the latest in appliances, bought a new car. The mimicry of salesman patter, classically that of a car salesman, is incomparable in this poem: "How about this suit——," "Believe me, they'll bury you in it" (bury him in his working clothes because work kills him in the prime of his life?); "I have the ticket for that"; "Well, what do you think of *that*?"; "A living doll, everywhere you look"; "It works, there is nothing wrong with it." The poem also makes special use of Plathian wordplay (a "crutch" and a "crotch" are both on sale), rhymes and near-rhymes ("crutch" and "crotch" again, "salt" and "suit," "fit" and "it," "proof" and "roof," "look," "cook," and "talk"), and repetitions (of "rubber" "no," "hand," "empty," "marry it," "talk"). Especially in such short, hortatory lines, this all sounds like a commercial jingle. The poem's voice is a salesman's in his emporium, but it is also a voice-over. In the commercial, an actor playing the consumer is supposed to pipe up with joyful responsion, but here one cue after another spews forth—yet nothing results but tears and then silence.

But the satire on different kinds of sales pitches, though it is deliciously funny, snags on the reader's mind, as does the sardonic fairy tale of victimization in "The Babysitters." Who *would* buy the interviewer/ therapist/salesman/advertiser's life-devouring tat? But as psychoanalytic theory plausibly claims, the will is intricate and multifaceted and changeable. Certainly in the beginning Plath and Hughes wanted each other very much, and for years they were mutually willing to concede what the other considered essential (including Hughes's freedom to cultivate male literary friendships, and childbearing for Plath). And they were both willing victims of whatever cultural blandishments (about romance and sex, the nuclear family, creature comforts, fame and prestige) fit in with their desires. The poem lampoons not only the monster of exploitative messaging, but also such easy victims, and on top of that their passive-aggressive displacement of their own wills. The voice is, after all, just a voice; it needs their consent. It cannot make them do anything. Plath can render the voice rivetingly, and very entertainingly, but she cannot control its influence on her life.

The biggest, most painful joke is that the originals of the two figures are both poets; the power of speaking belongs to them as gifted individuals. "It was the culture" or "It was you," or even "It was both of us, with one perverse, unacknowledged, intermeshed will," the disease of the double, does not cut any ice here.

For all of its ruefulness, open and implied, "The Applicant" is uplifting in its bold absurdity. Once again in reading Plath's poetry, I'm reminded of Terry Gilliam's animations. The blaring voice-over makes its loopy, unopposed pitches. Stiff, lifeless things that should be alive are summoned up and grotesquely manipulated. I can almost hear a huffing machine and can almost see it preparing to chop off body parts and stick on substitutes. Is the head shown as empty because it has been sliced across and opened like a lidded box?

But in the end, tragicomedy may be a truer impression of "The Applicant" than black comedy. Though the poem begins by implying substantial sympathy for the male interviewee, Plath is, as the lines wind down, writing more and more stingingly about herself. She is finally the "living doll," the all-around overperforming woman, the sort that the glossy magazines pledged could win back a bored or hostile husband, or one already on the way out, by becoming a better playmate and servant than her rival, or by just sitting on the shelf as long as it took him to see her value again.

The humiliation of this role for a woman like Plath

would have been profound. "[T]alk, talk, talk," the salesman's sneering description of the doll's mechanical chatter, abysmally demeans the doll-as-Plath; the human being has a serious calling to communicate. In the final stanza come frantic promises from the huckster, consonant with Plath's own racing, grandiose thoughts, reflected in her letters and conversations, about possibilities for winning her mate back. Forget the fakes and props at the poem's start: *she* is now the all-purpose filler for the man's emptinesses, he had better take her while he can, everything is at stake. But this is of course an oversell; he is still standing there. Why would he listen to the auctioneer-like chant of "Will you marry it, marry it, marry it"?

And if he does not listen, where will the surplus doll end up?

Ariel

OCTOBER 27, 1962

Stasis in darkness.
Then the substanceless blue
Pour of tor and distances.

God's lioness,
How one we grow,
Pivot of heels and knees!—The furrow

Splits and passes, sister to
The brown arc
Of the neck I cannot catch,

Nigger-eye
Berries cast dark
Hooks——

Black sweet blood mouthfuls,
Shadows.
Something else

Hauls me through air——
Thighs, hair;
Flakes from my heels.

White
Godiva, I unpeel——
Dead hands, dead stringencies.

And now I
Foam to wheat, a glitter of seas.
The child's cry

Melts in the wall.
And I
Am the arrow,

The dew that flies
Suicidal, at one with the drive
Into the red

Eye, the cauldron of morning.

IN *THE BELL JAR*, the protagonist Esther Greenwood is taken on a day trip to a ski resort in New England by the recovering tuberculosis patient and medical student she is supposed to marry. He does not know how to ski himself but applies theory, drills her in the rudiments, and sends her up the mountain on the tow rope, though she protests that she does not know how to "zigzag." He replies, "Oh, you need only go halfway. Then you won't gain very much momentum."

Despite fear, resentment, and the shameful mental picture of herself trudging down among the scrub pines with her skis off, Esther becomes whimsically calm: "The thought that I might kill myself formed in my mind coolly as a tree or a flower." She speeds down the slope, into what she perceives as a dark, tunnel-like space, and "through year after year of doubleness and smiles and compromises, into my own past," clear to "the white sweet baby cradled in its mother's belly." She crashes and breaks her leg, but demands another run.

In "Ariel," the title poem of Plath's renowned posthumous collection, the account of riding a runaway horse is elementally similar. But whereas the incident in the novel takes most of five pages, the poem is as fast as the core action; the poem does not even refer explicitly to riding, the horse, or the rider's thoughts and emotions; the reader has to build the situation up from mentions of isolated body parts, movements, perceptions, and sensations. *The Bell Jar* is far from sentimental, but it does incorporate some facile gestures at resolution. In this scene, the baby is the safe, perfect, untroubled narrator back in her mother's womb; the young woman plunges, as in lightning-fast psychoanalysis, toward that early vision of herself before the paralyzing conflicts of postpartum life intervene. The poems of Plath's last months dispense with this convention-weighted storytelling; even the love the speaker sometimes expresses for her children is open-ended, unaccountable. In "Ariel," an entire past, motherhood, children themselves are shed in a rush of terror and ecstasy too powerful to accommodate them; one child's cry is a fading sound in a left-behind room. At the end of the scene in *The Bell Jar*, as Esther lies in the snow, her boyfriend feeling her broken leg, she ignores the practicalities in favor of the ethereal: "A dispassionate white sun shone at the summit of the sky. I wanted to hone myself on it till I grew saintly and thin and essential as the blade of a knife." This language—note particularly the word "white" for purity—looks toward "Ariel," where prolonged, headlong flight transforms the speaker into another weapon, an arrow.

Other details of Plath's autobiography contribute even more specifically to the poem. When a fellow Cambridge student placed the inexperienced Plath on a horse, it bolted, and after a long, uncontrolled gallop she was stunned, bruised, and shaky, but she had clearly reexperienced the "passionately concentrated" feeling of the ski run. Also, around the time of the poem's composition, Plath took weekly rides on a horse named after Ariel, the magical "airy spirit" of Shakespeare's *The Tempest*.

Living in her Devon village's old manor house and riding for recreation, Plath might have seemed almost like a chatelaine—not the most comfortable role for an American expat teetering on the edge of divorce from an Englishman. (In "The Bee Meeting," written, like "Ariel," during that bleak October, the speaker meets the local worthies and thinks, "I am nude as a chicken neck, does nobody love me?" Her instincts are right: they end up ritually killing her.) The sole straightforward allusion in "Ariel" is to the medieval Lady Godiva, who according to legend rode, nude but cloaked in her long hair, through Coventry; her husband had made this the condition for repealing his new, oppressive taxes on their people. Trouble in a marriage can leave a woman terrifyingly exposed (some of Plath's perils at this period were physical, including illness; "Fever 103°" was written a week before) but can also help give her a place in history.

When she could, Plath would rise while it was still dark for a few hours of uninterrupted writing before her children woke and needed her attention. At these times, she wrote a number of masterpieces. Some of the poems look out the window at a dark and still scene that is inwardly alive and momentously engaged: at a talking, knowing tree, for example, that gallops all night and explodes ("Elm"), or at the moon that manifests womanhood, danger, and hostility. The predawn "stasis in darkness" in "Ariel" that for no stated reason becomes a headlong flight in one sense embodies paradoxes the poet lived day by day. Loneliness and blankness were opportunity, fear and despair were discovery, being left alone to care for a large home and small children was in a way the greatest freedom she had ever known, the possibility that she might not make it out alive was not the end of the world—if it was *her* world of art. She boasted in a letter to her mother that she was writing the poems that would make her name. They would, it must have been clear to her, survive her. At the end of "Ariel," the only thing ahead of the speaker is the rising sun—not so much the start of a day to live through as the "cauldron of morning" that will absorb the poet into its own smoldering alchemy. The sun reigns over life and itself lasts forever, because it is perfectly lifeless, nothing but energy. By this time—"Ariel" was written on her thirtieth birthday—Plath was heading toward personal disappearance and poetic immortality.

The poem's central metaphor is uplifting, transformative speed. I cast my mind back to standing in line again and again for turns on a moped at a teenage party: the machine surged magically, and I wondered every second whether I could keep control of it, but that made the ride more thrilling. We had nothing like this thing at home, and I kept seeking the sensation later through sports like white-water rafting and bodyboarding. Plath makes "Ariel" a sort of apotheosis of this impulse. In the poem, the urge engenders a miniature life story, clear from the "Stasis in darkness" as in the womb, instead of beginning at a glaring height and aiming childishly back before birth, in the way of *The Bell Jar*'s Esther. Instead of speeding back downward into a luckless victim's life, the "Ariel" persona merges with her mount, "God's lioness." (Is she caught up and carried away by a predator, not for ingestion but for an etherealizing sacrifice?) The two beings pass over the ground like a stream, tear through brambles that hook into the speaker's skin but do not slow her down, blend into a standing crop and then into the sea.

The Lady Godiva allusion that intervenes is like a springboard: by now the speaker has lost not only anything that covered and protected her but also the mount she had depended on for her forward movement: it is replaced by "Something else." Her body itself and all its habits and obligations, including her closest relationships ("Dead hands, dead stringencies," the crying child), rip away from her, with no resistance on her part. She finally resolidifies into an arrow, but only to become airborne, headed toward the rising sun, toward a "Suicidal" ending of the self that is an endless beginning.

In my introduction, I wrote of Plath getting a literary and rhetorical education of an intensity hardly known in the modern era. What probably intensified that privilege further, as in the case of Vergil and Horace, was that she came to it from quite a paltry and insecure place and so felt that she had to depend on it for her self-definition and prosperity. (And she added her husband, whose family had probably not dreamed of university for him when he was born, to the burden of her vocation: for all of his bitterness toward her after her suicide, he admitted that she had made him into a professional, famous poet. She initiated him into the literary marketplace, where he could make his otherworldliness itself a basis for conventional fame

and success.) From late childhood, Plath read, evalu-
ated, composed, in every way rehearsed literature. As
an undergraduate she pursued her craft and vocation
beyond her health and strength, without neglecting the
social and natural sciences. She often holed up to study
and write and went without sleep, to the puzzlement
and scorn of classmates for whom the Mrs. degree was
the height of aspiration. But the whole time, she also
dove into any other sources of new impressions that
were available: travel, sports, cultural events, an adven-
turous social life.

Though in evaluations of her character, Plath her-
self, seconded by her therapist, mother, husband, ene-
mies, and earlier biographers, often stressed the divided
self in terms that recall Freud—particularly concerning
the good-girl superego and alarming, angry id—a great
deal of evidence is to be had about her exhausting, self-
sacrificing explorations of the world, basically because
she was committed to rendering a notable, enduring
version of it.

The ancients subsumed the sciences and philosophy
under the practical heading of literature. Technical
knowledge came through carefully structured literary
works (including didactic poems) and was fed back
into them. Nautical, geographical, ethnographical, and
botanical information, and so on and on, was supposed
to be not only accurate but beautiful. Plath reflects this
immemorial ethic in a great number of poems, includ-
ing those about marine life, flowers, and bees, first see-

ing with razor-sharp clarity what she then sends into an imaginative storm. Even in such a sleek poem as "Ariel," she is dutiful toward physical reality and the precisions of common lore at the same time as she shakes personal existence off. The "tor" of the third line is a term derived from Old English for a high rocky hill. Plath did not know the term and paints with it merely because she was living in Britain; she had often hiked with her husband, a keen folklorist and nature lover, and as usual she had paid attention to everything and stashed up words and images. In Devon, where her home was, the Dartmoor upland is full of tors.

Likewise, the "Nigger-eye" berries are closely observed: blueberries and similar berries, especially when they are unripe, have a darker dot in the center, a little like the pupil of an eye.

But the greatest triumph of Plath's unstinting application was that she could achieve a masterpiece that looks effortless, as if created in the instinctive and only possible way. That capacity culminates, very fittingly, in this poem about wild release. "Ariel" is playful and artful, but the libraries and classrooms behind it are well concealed. To page through Plath's collected poems is to see many that are physically dense and extensive, and they are sometimes tiring to read, full of too many portentous stunts. "Ariel" starts with light wit, an economically phrased but double oxymoron of the landscape: the craggy hills are of course extremely solid, but the speaker's flight makes them flow like water and, even more, become as "substanceless" as the blue sky. The internal rhyme "Pour of tor" is striking, but it also flows rather than obtruding. Two short, verbless sentences—the speaker and the horse own the action already, and they are too fast to catch with a verb—make up the first stanza; with the motion well started, there is no further period until the middle of the fifth stanza. The images come clearly but in confusing relationship to each other, and rational syntax struggles, like the speaker trying to catch the horse's solid but bobbing neck. Four dashes in the poem do not so much interrupt the sequence of impressions as shatter it. Where the sentences are textbook-grammatical and narrative, what is conveyed is increasingly, and ironically, dissolution. The "I" "foam[s]" into featureless standing wheat, the child's cry of human appeal and connection, or just of memory, "melts," even "The dew . . . flies / Suicidal." As if resisting, the "I" is repeatedly emphasized by expanding to whole short lines ("And now I"; "And I"), only to undergo a final self-annihilating transformation, into the arrow that leaves the accountable world. Cleverly, the final stanza and the additional, separate final line are assimilated with long "i" sounds, the I now being not I but part of "flies," "Suicidal," "drive," and the crowning "eye," a sound identical to "I": the self has become pure vision.

The "eye" almost at the end of the poem is the evanescence of the earthy and transgressively named

"Nigger-eye"—the adjective's obtrusiveness enhanced by its position as a whole line beginning a stanza. In emphasizing Plath's learning and her application to her craft, I may seem to slight her rebellion and anger. But I like to consider these, along with other things, in their literary context and use. I ask readers to take the following whence it comes and indulge a classicist, but Plath's work really does make more sense to me not as a throwback, of course, but as a new vindication of a very long tradition. The ancients were quite practical about literature; they used what they had, not begrudging beautiful and refined forms to ugly subjects and moods. In poetry, rage, obscenity, and insult had their own proper genres with their own meters, their own music and dance in some cases, and a number of sanctioned settings and occasions for performance. This is not to say that this literature always went over well, or reliably floated over predictable consequences (a target of Aristophanes's verse sued him, a target of Archilochus's is said to have hanged himself). But such literature did have a special sphere for self-expression that it lost in eras of greater propriety and social and political self-consciousness. (I am not going to use the term "political correctness," which refers to a specific set of current taboos.) Plath *was* a throwback inasmuch as she would not deny herself the exact effects she wanted for fear of offending; usually the offense helped to make her point, as in "Daddy": if you *want* to show your rage bouncing out of control, you can't do much better than a childish, black-humor comparison of yourself to victims of the Holocaust.

Authors with startling aesthetic achievements have traditionally enjoyed some protection against moral judgments—not that Plath is in dire need of that protection. She was a doctrinaire progressive of her era, and generally a civilized person; she did not belittle the Holocaust in conversation; she did not use the N-word on the street. But like "Daddy," "Ariel" is a poem of final departure: the shocking term "Nigger-eye" certainly gets the reader's attention, but it does so for the calculated purpose of renouncing present things for a life beyond. The darkness, the standing crops that would be tawny, the brown horse's neck, the dark berries that recall the eyes of people who toiled in American fields against their will, are all what the white, pure, increasingly weightless Godiva, the woman who is heading toward full release and becoming a ghost, is leaving; color, especially dark color, stands for solidity, the stain of use and habit, the whole familiar earth, and white is emptiness, cloud, the clean, blank page on which something wonderful may still be written. By using an offensive term in making this contrast, the poet is shaking off, along with all other burdens of her mortal life, personal judgments of herself. This is not a dinner party (in Plath's life, in fact, literary social life had thinned out after her separation from Hughes); when she writes poetry, she is not afraid of losing friends. And in her

literary existence she is simply incapable of the kind of
offense that comes from sheer carelessness or obnox-
iousness. There is eyewitness confirmation that she
hogged the caviar at a *Mademoiselle* reception; she con-
fesses to picking her nose in libraries and smearing up
shared books; but she wrote fine passages about both
scenes, one in *The Bell Jar* and one in her journal. The
"Nigger-eye" berries are well-placed, economical, very
evocative. They embody the theme—the message of
the medium—that she was pouring her personality and
consciousness into literature, with diminishing concern
for anything else.

I take the word "Suicidal" in the same sense. Surely a
simplistic autobiographical interpretation of the word
impoverishes the poem. I also think that such a reading
may be biographically inaccurate. The facts around her
suicide leave it unclear whether she had been intend-
ing a mere suicidal gesture. Plath left a message to con-
tact her doctor, who had finally secured her a bed in
an excellent facility. It may be that she could not wait
for her admission, or wanted to be sure her case was
treated seriously. Her interactions with her neighbor
the night before strongly suggest that she meant him to
be the front line of her rescue, and he probably would
have been had the gas not seeped through to his flat,
knocking him out.

But much more important for a critic to consider is
the virtuoso performance of the *Ariel* poems amid the
pain Plath was enduring. A friend she was staying with

tried to get her to tend more readily to her children, but she had a classical symptom of severe depression: she sometimes physically couldn't move. Yet around the same time she was doing literary work that required hours of disciplined and acute concentration. Hers is not the typical story of a suicide, about the loss of hope in what is most important—whereas her youthful suicide attempt came about in just this way: she could not write, and complained of that. Toward the end of her life, Plath wrote much of her best work, and was sometimes exhilarated and proud. She knew she had arrived, so what is this flight of departure in "Ariel"? I would call the "suicide" the painful, terrifying, thrilling, irrevocable gift of her life to her writing; and I would call the release the speaker feels not the peace of death but the confidence of immortality.

Edge

FEBRUARY 5, 1963

The woman is perfected.
Her dead

Body wears the smile of accomplishment,
The illusion of a Greek necessity

Flows in the scrolls of her toga,
Her bare

Feet seem to be saying:
We have come so far, it is over.

Each dead child coiled, a white serpent,
One at each little

Pitcher of milk, now empty.
She has folded

Them back into her body as petals
Of a rose close when the garden

Stiffens and odors bleed
From the sweet, deep throats of the night flower.

The moon has nothing to be sad about,
Staring from her hood of bone.

She is used to this sort of thing.
Her blacks crackle and drag.

"EDGE" may be the last poem of Sylvia Plath's life. It was written six days before her suicide in February 1963, along with "Balloons," a typically clever object poem about "Oval soul-animals," a magical treasure of delight. But the final two stanzas of the six in "Balloons" turn ominous. The speaker is, by now at least, addressing an older child about her baby brother's antics: he makes his balloon "squeak like a cat," gazes through it as if at a "funny pink world he might eat," bites it, then sits back like a "fat jug"; before him now to contemplate is "a world clear as water," and he has "A red / Shred in his little fist."

A closely autobiographical interpretation is irresistible here. Plath struggled to connect with her children when she was depressed. "I'm no more your mother / Than the cloud" reflected in but disappearing over the rain puddle it created, says the mother in "Morning Song," written a few weeks before Frieda's first birthday. It is easy to read in "Balloons," dating near the end of the poet's life, hostility toward Nicholas, the child whose birth was much harder and who fell into a marriage already in trouble. In "Balloons," he destroys through his instinct to grasp and feed, reducing an enchanting, metaphorically living thing to a negligible scrap the color of blood. The poem also suggests a suicide's typical calculation that those close to her will be better off if she is gone. No noise registers as the balloon is popped, and anyway the baby can now gaze undisturbed at the unfiltered, unimpeded world, oblivious to what he has lost. The balloons are, after all, just leftovers from festivities; the mother's poetic giftedness, which cherishes and transforms the balloons in *her* eyes, amounts to little in reality right here, though she has treated her calling as central to her life. If the children are not equipped to appreciate and therefore miss her identity in this sense, will they really miss her?

"Edge" meditates more directly than "Balloons" on the fate of a suicide's children. Here they are not only dead (appearing more lifeless than the mother), but also merged back into her body; yet, strangely, she is not a cool, ironic-sounding observer of her offspring, as in the other poem: instead, the process of taking them with her has been like the natural autumn wilting of a fragrant garden to the senses of someone who loves it—the gardener? Plath and Hughes had gardened on the grounds of their home. A friendly journalist had visited there, and the resulting feature included a photo of Plath seated among the daffodils with her two children.

The first half of the poem, however, has a setting reminiscent of the ancient world. Plath had been impressed with certain images of the proto-surrealist painter Giorgio de Chirico: robed, statuelike female figures appear near arched buildings in bleak twilight landscapes. In a painting after which Plath named a poem of 1957, "The Disquieting Muses," one figure is upright, the other seated, and both have smooth knobs for heads. The figures are, to the poem's speaker, the fairy tale–like curse-bearers at her christening, the embodiment of the mother's controlling, falsifying, paralyzing treatment of the daughter's potential.

Another poem of the same year, "All the Dead Dears," is about a fourth-century sarcophagus with a woman's remains in it. A mouse and a shrew were shut in as well, and one or both gnawed the corpse's ankle before their own deaths: their skeletons were exhibited with hers in a museum, witnesses, according to Plath, to "the gross eating game." The speaker perceives genera-tions of women "reach[ing] hag hands to haul me in" to the coffin too, and the tough-minded journey through everything—"weddings, / Childbirths or a family bar-becue"—toward this place of annihilation.

In "Edge," however, all horror movie–type terror and resistance are gone, and classical calm and beauty reign. Though the subject of this poem is explicitly a "dead / Body," it does not show any decay or damage or a repellent rictus; in a photo, the skeleton that inspired "All the Dead Dears" is open-mouthed as if still in its dying agony. Plath's dead woman is, in contrast, "per-fected," with a "smile of accomplishment" and neat "scrolls of her toga."

The toga is the Roman civic uniform, and its point

is male self-presentation. Its heavy, long dips of drap-
ery ("scrolls" is nice here, as if the figure is wearing
ancient literature) did not allow for physical work and
made living emblems out of men doing public busi-
ness. De Chirico's female figures, and women depicted
in ancient art, wear feminine drapery, so I am inclined
to think that Plath's use of "toga" here is deliberate, in
spite of the phrase "illusion of a Greek necessity" and
other allusions to Greek tragedy in the poem. Plath
was almost never actually careless (as opposed to pur-
posefully choppy and eclectic) in assembling her imag-
ery. I therefore think that the dead body is more like
an upright monument—say, a sculpture of a Roman
orator—than a supine corpse, and that the "smile of
accomplishment" is the conscious satisfaction with
deserved immortality, as great as any man's. Fittingly,
her feet remain alive enough to testify to the length
of their journey toward becoming this very special
memorial.

Interestingly, her dead children, as curled-up "white
serpent[s]," are more transformed, more purely sym-
bolic than she, the commanding central figure; and
in their greater distance from their living selves, they
are strikingly subsidiary to her. Yet the images seem
to meld with the real children in accordance with the
plan Plath would carry out in a few days. The children
would wake up to terror and confusion, their mother
not there; instead, there would be solemn, minimally
communicative acquaintances and strangers, and their

overwrought father. The bread (homemade?) and
fresh milk that Plath had set out where the children
could get to them represented an effort to distract and
comfort them for a time, and to stretch her presence
as a nurturer a little longer. In the poem "For a Father-
less Son," she had written, "You will be aware of an
absence, presently, / Growing beside you. . . ." What if
the female side of parentage went blank for them too?
"Edge" acknowledges that she will leave a dire gap, that
the pitchers will be empty.

But there is a great difference between the pathetic
skeleton rodents of "All the Dead Dears" and the dead
serpent-children of "Edge." The younger, childless
speaker in the first poem sees the movement between
generations as pitiful and pitiless; the mother in "Edge,"
in contrast, needs to leave her children something and
to picture them at a sort of peace with her loss. Her
children must, at least, not be gnawing her corpse, as it
were, trapped in her death like negligible tiny animals:
they are a formal, proper part of her monument, not a
cruel accident.

On a ritual level, the coiled snakes beside empty
pitchers of milk may reflect the ancient custom of food
offerings to the dead, whose spirits were sometimes
pictured in the form of snakes, spirits of the earth's and
the underworld's lowly-seeming but essential power.
For a snake to actually appear in the open, drink the
milk from the offering bowl, and disappear again into
its hole was highly propitious, as it meant that the

dead person's spirit was appeased and would cause no
trouble. I find this interpretation more plausible than
an allusion to the asp by which Cleopatra committed
suicide; but Robert Graves in *The White Goddess* does
associate the deity of his title with Cleopatra, and liter-
ary mystics of Plath's generation, including Plath, were
devoted to his book. And in Shakespeare's *Antony and
Cleopatra*, the queen commits suicide with two asps and
says, as she picks up the first one, "Dost thou not see
my baby at my breast / That sucks the nurse asleep?"
There is of course no necessity for either-or choices
between readings, but I think funerary offerings better
suit the guilt and fear of a mother of two small children
who is about to attempt, if not suicide outright, then an
extremely risky suicidal gesture. The whole affect of
the poem, however, is admittedly against the biograph-
ical argument that Plath meant to live and fight on; but
there would be nothing uncharacteristic in her feeling
both ways in the same hour and imprinting both feel-
ings in the same poem.

There is at any rate no facile solution to the de-
existential dilemma the poem presents. If the children
are spirits of the dead that have been propitiated, they
do not disappear into the underworld. The woman has
taken them back into her own body in a reverse birth.
It is a shocking exercise of her power; the process as
presented, however, is not gruesome and forced but
beautiful and natural. She is, if not a gardener, then a
garden out of season ("the garden / Stiffens")—England

was at the time enduring the worst cold and snow in decades—frozen and rigid but still fragrant and holding the promise of regeneration. Also, some flowers, like these, open at night, emitting uncanny perfume "From the sweet, deep throats"; some poetry flourishes only after the poet's death, along with her legend.

Underlying the poem thematically is tragedy, a genre that Plath studied at Cambridge, and that influenced both her and Hughes greatly. In Euripides's *Medea*, the eponymous sorceress queen kills her two children to punish her deserting husband and throws the corpses down to him from the flying chariot in which she flees. By "The illusion of a Greek necessity," I understand a reference to long-standing arguments— staple classroom fare—about the way tragic plots work. Are they the diagrams of fate's machine, or tales of free human choices? Does "illusion" here signal that, even if there is no way out for the victims, there is a way out in another sense? Greek tragedy was in its origins a fertility ritual and remained a celebration of many joyful things: at the festivals where tragedies were enacted, the whole community came together for drinking, eating, dancing, music, and patriotic observances, as well as for literature. Individuals go under, but the spectacles don't; nor do the work and the memory of those who create the spectacles.

Plath was deeply superstitious, capable of reading a sign in nature or an everyday example of asinine male behavior to mean that her husband would leave her and she would die, and she was liable to then go ahead and help seal her fate with her own behavior. For instance, as her jealous rage grew, she burned many of Hughes's papers and her own, and probably also some of his personal detritus such as fingernails, and later told associates, including at least one unsympathetic one (apt to report to Hughes in scathing terms), about the scary rituals. Such incidents can make her look like the classic tragic protagonist for whom a flawed character is a built-in fate. But there was a stronger side to her that shrugged off tragedy in this more mundane sense, or she would not have kept writing until almost the end of her life. She knew she had an emanating throat like the night flowers in "Edge," a source of unforgettable and thus self-renewing words.

The moon is a cold, hostile, and controlling mother figure in other poems. In "The Moon and the Yew Tree" the moon is "White as a knuckle and terribly upset," gaping in comprehensive dismay and dragging the entire sea after her; in "Elm," "The moon, also, is merciless: she would drag me [the spirit of the deeply rooted elm] / Cruelly, being barren." In "Edge," however, the moon drags only her own surrounding darkness, like garments so stiff and heavy that they "crackle." I used to find that final line disappointing, with its relative flatness and obscurity amid so many of simple magnificence in the poem, and amid so many mesmerizing moon images in the Plath oeuvre; also, the sounds here become quite ugly: "blacks," "crackle," drag." But there is a thematic function in this off-putting trailing off. The moon has lost her poetic power: it has all been transferred to the dead woman. The heavenly body can only make her slow, lonely way across heaven like an overdressed, sidelined mourner.

There is now no cringing below her, no brooding blame aimed up at her. She is staring like a stranger from her skull-like "hood of bone": what should be the utter nakedness of skinlessness is a barrier of cronelike clothing; this creature was never going to be approachable and appeasable. She is now brushed off by two of Plath's most stunning colloquial lines: "The moon has nothing to be sad about" and "She is used to this sort of thing." These words echo the kind of passive aggression heard in comic dialogue: "Don't mind *me*: this is just what I have to put up with all the time." This is the tone of a frustrated, peevish old woman, not of a demon.

Plath's most plentiful real-world inspiration for her moon imagery was of course her own mother. At this period Aurelia, as she admitted later, was feeling some despair for her own sake. It must indeed have looked as if she would never get out from under the care of an adult child with, after all, far more opportunities than her mother had had, a daughter who should have been able to get on with challenging responsibilities according to her mother's example but instead bounced between grandiose views of her future and demands for material help.

Plath for her part may have realized that she was out on the cliff-edge of a dependent relationship. She had worn out other support too. In her rages and panics of the summer and fall of 1962, as an effect of illness, exhaustion, anger, and a wounded ego, she had achieved a sort of fugue state of self-centeredness. She wrote "Lady Lazarus," in which the speaker is an artist of suicide as striptease, riveting a "peanut-crunching crowd" and selling pieces of her body like a perverted saint. She expected her brother's new wife to come to England to care for her and her children. She tried to land as a lover a literary man and friend of Hughes's she should have known would smugly and censoriously gossip about the episode. She installed and quickly turned on an au pair. She seethed at alarmed, overburdened hosts when she could not cope with staying home.

"Edge," however, testifies to a very different mood. Ironically, the single figure's utter domination of the scene—her children reduced to snake carcasses, her now negligible moon-mother writing her off like one relative among many gone to the dogs—gives her a clean impersonality and an ability to observe dispassionately yet speak eloquently. What she observes now is the self that cannot be taken away from her, the beauty of her achievement: "The woman is perfected."

It feels almost heartless, in the face of the tragedies that unfolded from Plath's demise—including the murder-suicide of her rival, Assia Wevill, who took her four-year-old daughter by Hughes along with her, and the suicide of Plath's son in middle age—to speak of her poems as her most beloved children, who inherited endless further growing seasons, which she had determinedly provided for them. But that is probably the truer story. As I wrote before, Plath's poems, whatever their other subjects, are disproportionately about writing poetry; and this theme, along with others, is deeply embedded in the structure. Here, comparatively short lines, typical signals of sharp pain, final loss, disappointment, and dismissal, *refer* to the physical and mortal, but *start* sentences about much more. "Her dead / Body wears the smile of accomplishment"; "Her bare / Feet seem to be saying: / We have come so far, it is over."

Throughout "Edge," a calm observer speaks for the dead woman, except in the moment when her feet give their message: "We have come so far, it is over." They are bare, stripped of their earthly accoutrements (in the ancient world, taking shoes off, unbinding hair, and other acts of divestiture might be required before entering holy ground), exhausted from their journey; but they are part of her, and so speak with a ghostly authority: they testify that the life is "over"; but "come so far" has a double meaning: a long, punishing journey, fit to complain of, but also a mighty advance, an achievement. Plath had come far indeed. "Edge" is less a dirge than a celebratory performance of her literary immortality.

Recommendations for Further Reading

Tracy Brain, ed. *Sylvia Plath in Context*. Cambridge, UK: Cambridge University Press, 2019.

Heather Clark. *Red Comet: The Short Life and Blazing Art of Sylvia Plath*. New York: Knopf, 2020.

Jo Gill, ed. *The Cambridge Companion to Sylvia Plath*. Cambridge, UK: Cambridge University Press, 2006.

Anita Helle, Amanda Golden, and Maeve O'Brien, eds. *The Bloomsbury Handbook to Sylvia Plath*. London: Bloomsbury Academic, 2022.

Sylvia Plath. *Ariel: The Restored Edition*. New York: Harper Perennial, 2018.

Sylvia Plath. *The Bell Jar*. London: Heinemann, 1963.

Sylvia Plath. *The Collected Poems*. New York: Harper Perennial, 2018.

Sylvia Plath. *The Letters of Sylvia Plath* (2 vols.), edited by Peter K. Steinberg and Karen V. Kukil. New York: Harper, 2017–2018.

Sylvia Plath. *The Unabridged Journals of Sylvia Plath*, edited by Karen V. Kukil. New York: Vintage, 2000.

Jacqueline Rose. *The Haunting of Sylvia Plath*. London: Virago UK, 2014.

Andrew Wilson. *Mad Girl's Love Song: Sylvia Plath and Life Before Ted*. New York: Scribner, 2013.

Elizabeth Winder. *Pain, Parties, Work: Sylvia Plath in New York, Summer 1953*. New York: HarperCollins, 2014.

Acknowledgments

I heartily thank my editor, Stefanie Peters, who dreamed this book into being, seeking me out and persuading me to have the critical adventure of a lifetime. And Stefanie came along on the adventure, lending learned and patient help in every difficulty. Through her good offices, I also obtained very useful advice from eminent scholars of contemporary literature Amanda Golden and Stephanie Burt as well as one anonymous reader.

To my husband Tom Conroy and my agent Gail Hochman, I quote Queen: "Ooh you make me live." For the University of Pennsylvania Classics Department, it's "Ooh you let me read." Without the department's generous, long-term research support, I would not be writing any books.

About the Author

SARAH RUDEN is a poet, a translator of ancient literature, and a writer about literature and the history of ideas. She has a Harvard doctorate in Latin and Greek and spent a decade in Africa, where she taught at the University of Cape Town, volunteered for the South African Education and Environment Project, and won the Central News Agency Literary Award for her poetry collection *Other Places*. She has translated Vergil's *Aeneid*, Aristophanes' *Lysistrata*, Augustine's *Confessions*, and other works, and has published books about the Bible (*Paul Among the People* and *The Face of Water*) and a biography of Vergil. Her biography of the martyr Perpetua is forthcoming from Yale University Press, and from Norton her survey of anti-family-planning messaging since the first century BCE. The Guggenheim, Whiting, and Silvers Foundations have supported her work.

This book is set in 10⅞ point Weiss, a digital typeface reissued by Linotype from the Weiss Antiqua typeface designed in 1928 by German poet, painter, and graphic artist Emil Rudolf Weiß (1875–1942) for the Bauer Foundry of Frankfurt. Weiß created numerous fonts during the 1920s and early 1930s before his teaching credentials were revoked by the Nazi regime in 1933, after which he retired to his home in in Baden-Baden. The display elements are set in Canela, a typeface that, inspired by the art of stone-carving, is neither purely serif nor sans serif; it was drawn by Miguel Reyes and published through Commercial Type in 2016.

The paper is acid-free and exceeds the requirements for permanence established by the American National Standards Institute.

Text design and composition by Gopa & Ted2, Inc., Albuquerque, NM.

Printing by Maple Press, York, PA.